IN HER
OWN
WORDS

For my mother, Susanna

i.m. Anne Cluysenaar
1936-2014

IN HER OWN WORDS

Women Talking Poetry and Wales

Interviewed by
Alice Entwistle

Foreword by Gillian Clarke

SEREN

Seren is the book imprint of
Poetry Wales Press Ltd
Nolton Street, Bridgend, Wales

www.serenbooks.com
facebook.com/SerenBooks
Twitter: @SerenBooks

ISBN 978-1-78172-202-2
Epub 978-1-78172-203-9
Mobi 978-1-78172-204-6

A CIP record for this title is available from the British Library

The publisher works with the financial assistance
of the Welsh Books Council

Printed by Bell & Bain Ltd, Glasgow

CONTENTS

FOREWORD

From the talk-talk in English and Welsh in the crowded family house where I was born, there was never a minute without language being the very breath of life – nursery rhymes, bedtime stories, my mother speaking the common names of wild flowers, my father's telling the great myths of the Mabinogi on every slow drive west to the family farm in Pembrokeshire. His sister, my aunt, a railway clerk who educated herself through reading, took me to my first Shakespeare play. I was ten. It was King Lear. I will never forget the big, pantomime thrill of it, and some of the lines echo still.

Because of bedtime stories, and libraries – no parent could provide a pile of new books every week – I was an early reader, a book-worm. I have always kept a journal. It is the physicality of language itself, not ideas in the head, that drives poetry. In both poetry and prose it is the word-music that inspires, the loping syntax, the song in a line. Formal education offered only poetry by men, and all of them English. There was never a Welsh character in any story. As a Welsh girl I had no poet-heroines to follow. At the time of writing, my three colleague Poets Laureate are women. They voice the world with a new music. The voices of all poets, dead and alive, men and women, keep poetry singing, and, in a young century, reaching a wider audience than ever.

Gillian Clarke

INTRODUCTION

Anthologies cannot but mark their moment. In our age of digital mobility email, social media sites and the tools of social engagement which they bring us, channelled through the chronically insomniac android phone, wire us into ever-denser tangles of encounter and inter-relation. The burgeoning of our digital social lives gives onto concerns I needn't rehearse here, but are perhaps offset by one kind of consolation. If nothing else, Facebook, Twitter, Skype and the rest seem heartening confirmation of human society's prizing of exchange, remote or otherwise. It might sometimes seem that we risk losing as much as we gain from being ceaselessly in touch, and so often in a textual halfworld of abbreviation: atm, tbh, gr8. But perhaps digitized forms of social encounter make other versions of human exchange, conducted in more traditional and permanent-feeling contexts or registers, seem more precious. Perhaps they leave us the keener to seek out and savour the kinds of conversation chronicled here.

Every book trails a history. *In Her Own Words* is rooted in the critical survey of poetry by women in contemporary Wales which I published last year, itself grown in the more comprehensive historical survey of twentieth-century British women poets which I co-wrote with Jane Dowson before it.[1] It was in researching and writing the latter work that I came fully to appreciate the vibrancy of Wales' contemporary poetry, and the scholarship it merited. As critics have noticed, women have been writing poetry in Wales for centuries; if their contribution to an already dynamic poetry scene since about 1970 hadn't been overlooked, neither –

in 2005 – had their work attracted the kind of close attention
which their counterparts in Scotland and Ireland were by then
enjoying.[2] There was a distinct disparity between the warm interest of reviewers, and the comparatively limited critical
scholarship available on the same writers. There were no
monographs; few of the available essays and book chapters were
even single-author studies. Apart from reviews, that left profiles
and features, and an uneven scattering of interviews.

The pattern was not unfamiliar to me, nor was it gender-
specific: there have always been many more good poets than
scholars writing about them. But I could see in the real-time
story I was uncovering in Wales the invigorating opportunity, for
once, to do more than merely record and lament it. Here was a
chance to help alter the arc; to generate the kind of broader and
more nuanced scholarship the poets deserved. I had the contract
for the critical study. Undertaking a series of interviews alongside
it, with some of the writers whose work I was planning to
examine, seemed an obvious next step. I'd long been in the habit
of interviewing my subjects if I could. I didn't pause to think
about it.

*

Like the monograph it took shape alongside, *In Her Own Words*
aims both to register and respond to the poets' creative achievements, and to the variform poetic landscape they have helped
shape down the years in Wales, in and through publications like
Poetry Wales, *New Welsh Review* and *Planet*. As I hope what follows
will make plain, as much divides my cast of interlocutors as
connects them. A visit to the poems should of course rapidly
confirm the nature and extent of the creative space/s between the
writers represented here, irrespective of the ground covered by
my conversations with them. Yet it seems worth pointing out the
breadth of the geography on which the book draws, extending –
outside Wales – from Dublin to Shetland to Suffolk; and – within
Wales – from the mountainous interior and coastal edges of
Gwynedd via Ceredigion and Powys, to rural Usk, south to

Cardiff and east to Newport. The extent of that terrain suggests the difficulties of confining the dimensions of Wales' lively creative life within any too-precise territorial map. The contributors range almost as broadly in age and, of course, in experience and outlook. However, as professional writers of course, there is naturally a good degree of occupational overlap between them. Writing remains a precarious way of making a living on its own; if most of the poets have found other ways to support themselves, only a few have not been involved in some form of teaching at some time in their lives, many in higher education.

In terms of poetic subject matter, and predictably, the poets featured here pursue different thematic concerns for different reasons, and from different angles. Their attitudes to matters of form, to the handling of voice, genre, narrative and/or other kinds of raw material markedly vary. Likewise their reading tastes; their interest in other writers, especially other poets; and above all, unsurprisingly, their sense of creative direction. For all those disparities, however, the interviews together tour the manifold and complex links between geography, political and/or literary cultures, and poetry. The encounters were never constructed – by me or the writers – in any kind of adversarial way, as some kinds of interview are: theatre, revelation, discomfort had no place in the kind of exploratory exchanges I sought. I wanted simply to ensure that sooner or later any discussion paused, specifically, on what it is to find yourself writing poetry, as a woman, in the complex, contested literary space marking the Wales of now, or recently. On what it is – in public, professional and creative terms – to find yourself, as a woman, actively helping to shape a creative nation's long-lived, self-reinventing poetic history. On what it might mean to write poetry in either language of that layered cultural terrain, to contribute to an aesthetic as well as actual *topos* always alert – and interestedly retuning itself – to the shifts and slippages of its changing political shape. What writers you read, and what writers help you write; how poems take shape, and what they might be good for; how to negotiate the role of the self – as daughter, mother, companion, wife – in the poem itself, but also in the life outside and beyond it. What Wales looks like, to a poet writing out of its layered cultural melange; what it might in all its complexities be transformed into, in and by the conversational spaces of the (exclusively female-authored) poetic text.

A lover of many kinds of poetry – not only by women, not only by living writers, and certainly not only from or about Wales – I also wanted to make sure that discussions ranged as far or wide as a poet wanted to go; to tap the conversational riches of contingency, surprise or digression. Thus on the whole I avoided sending lists of questions in advance, preferring to prepare writers by explaining the context for my interest in them, describing the vision of the monograph, and suggesting two or three possible areas of discussion. Routing the conversation into questions of form and its use was always a central priority, and seemed to be relished by the writers; the role and function of the lyric sequence became something of a general navigation point.

Among a range of more ideological topics, I specifically wanted to probe the issue of gender, its importance or otherwise in today's Wales, and in contemporary literary/poetic culture as a whole, where poets were receptive. Not all were. That said, if some were reluctant to concede the effect of their gender on the shape and nature of their own writing careers, few were prepared to sidestep the fact of their shared womanhood, still less gainsay its circumstantial relevance to their home and/or working lives. Overall, however, among this admittedly tiny sample of writers, the possibility that gender might exert any discernible influence on the workings of the poetic imaginary remained largely moot. Finally, if biographical stories take their place among the other kinds of narratives which different conversations incorporate, neither, I hope, will they seem to predominate.

★

Here, then, are the voices of fourteen powerful poets, all identifying (and to a greater or less extent identified by others) with Wales, reflecting with often humorous insight on their creative interests and practices; their thinking and writing lives; their relationships with different kinds of readers; their different, often complicated cultural contexts. Thus the sharp-eyed but self-effacing Ruth Bidgood, in her ninth decade uncontested *doyenne* of contemporary Wales' poetic scene; thus the Welsh-speaking, Pembrokeshire-bred, Dublin-domiciled Nerys Williams, among the newest of the voices to make itself heard in recent years. Nearby stand two of the most active, and widely-respected, figures of Wales' robust bilingual literary and political life, Menna Elfyn and Gwyneth Lewis, both of them earthed, inventive and increasingly influential poetic models: both at ease on an international stage, both sought-after global ambassadors for their nation and language. Here, Belgian-born Anne Cluysenaar, writing out of the Usk countryside, and her friend the passionately Wales-identifying Wendy Mulford, based in rural Suffolk, keep suggestive company with contemporaries like Sheenagh Pugh, now writing out of Shetland; Christine Evans, whose farming family divides the year between Bardsey Island and the mainland Pen Llŷn; Newport native Catherine Fisher and the American émigré Anne Stevenson. Each is a veteran, in her own way, of another kind of literary community. And beside these, finally, some of the accomplished path-breakers of a successive generation are brought into view: Deryn Rees-Jones, Samantha Wynne-Rhydderch, Zoë Skoulding and Tiffany Atkinson.

It would be disingenuous, however, to suggest that this record of those voices is an uncomplicated one. Any text which centralizes the figure of the author needs treating with caution: authorship is in its own way a performance, always under construction in response to different kinds of stimuli. How differentiate the real-life novelist-self we might trace through her journals, letters, or memoirs from, say, any of her fictional creations? The same creative consciousness and the same slippery language are at work in both kinds of text; why trust either over the other? Since by definition perspective is limited, what textual 'I', fictional or not, could ever hope to tell the 'full story' about itself?

Beside these kinds of textual instabilities, the spontaneities of speech seem enticingly honest. The genre of the interview knowingly draws on this power: it promises us the unrehearsed utterance, brings the horse's mouth appealingly near. Talk can't take refuge in disguise: it rambles, interrupts, contradicts, *gives itself away*. Yet those same provisionalities (as prone to misprision as misuse, as Stephen Connor reminds us: 'What I say goes,') are precisely what help to make the interview a treacherous terrain[3]. Any interview offers a record; it depends for its existence on preserving the said, what would otherwise 'go' or be lost. Ironically in fact, however, it can only conserve the precious spontaneities of speech by transforming them into fixities; talk does not turn into text, specifically, without the layers of inter-vention involved in transcription, editing, trimming. Poised ambivalently between the apparently 'authentic' record of an encounter and its always belated textual confection, the interview encompasses a process of interchange and negotiation from initial overture to final approval. In all its temporal, socio-geographical and material particularities, it is difficult to see how an interviewee's 'I' can seem any less constructed than any other.

This project foregrounds these instabilities in one more way. Typically, conversations took place as (digitally) recorded face-to-face encounters, before being transcribed, edited and shaped by email into the versions reproduced here. Not all worked like this. A conversation with Christine Evans which began at a conference in Gregynog continued in voice-files recorded by the poet in response to a series of follow-up questions; it was a consolingly conversation-like solution which satisfied us both. Three more (with Sheenagh Pugh, Anne Stevenson and Nerys Williams) were conducted exclusively by email, mostly question by question, but with all the artificialities that remote communi-cation entails. However, the longevity of the project complicates this history. Since the interviewing process began back in 2006, several authors were keen to revise their versions (including the one or two already in print) before the transcript was finally submitted in the late spring of 2014.

Arguably, its lengthy genesis makes this book seem both less stable and more nuanced, its life-history warning us against assuming too much of an apparently 'authentic' authorial voice.

Revising her own interview some years after it took place, Zoë Skoulding amusedly casts her defamiliarised, bi-temporal voice as a 'palimpsest', its twinned versions of itself both underpinning and overwriting each other in an unexpectedly effective representation of her changed and changing creative consciousness. It seems a helpful response. Authors are people; people's views vary, from hour to hour, day to day, week to week. Can identity ever be fixed, textually or otherwise? What part does consistency play in selfhood or subjectivity, other than in the rarified world of the literary creation? *In Her Own Words* may seem to approach a kind of accuracy in its silent signposting of the complexities I've been outlining. Yet I remain hopeful that the conversations offer readers both a clear sense of the distinct, variegated, articulate *poet* in each interlocutor, and access to a more choric – collective – voice, both testifying to the imaginative riches on which the cultural repository of Wales, our shared geo-political hinterland, opens.

As Deryn Rees-Jones points out, any poem marks the traces of an intensely private-public conversation conducted between text, word and poet. That conversation in turn implicitly reaches out in all directions towards the kinds of conversation on which centuries of writing and reading – of exchange between writers, texts and readers – make possible. Poems have an irrepressible habit of drawing into conversation any unsuspecting passer-by who happens to pause near them: any kind of voice can contribute to their inexhaustible, contingent, conversational life. What better hope than that this book and the encounters it offers might encourage new readers to make their own visit to the terrain it surveys; to begin mapping for themselves the restive, generative dialogue between poetry, place and identity?

Alice Entwistle
April 2014

---

1. Alice Entwistle, *Poetry, Geography, Gender: Women re-writing contemporary Wales* (Cardiff: University of Wales Press, 2013); Jane Dowson and Alice Entwistle, *A History of Twentieth Century British Women's Poetry*

(Cambridge University Press, 2005).

2. See *Welsh Women's Poetry 1460-2001: An Anthology*, ed. Katie Gramich and Catherine Brennan (Dinas Powys: Honno Classics, 2003); *Sleeping with Monsters: Conversations with Scottish and Irish Women Poets*, ed. Gillean Somerville-Arjat and Rebecca E. Wilson (Edinburgh: Polygon, 1991).

3. Stephen Connor, *Dumbstruck: A Cultural History of Ventriloquism* (Oxford University Press, 2000), 7.

TIFFANY ATKINSON

Tiffany Atkinson is the author of three full-length collections of poetry: *Kink and Particle* (Seren, 2006), *Catulla et al* (Bloodaxe, 2011) and *So Many Moving Parts* (Bloodaxe, 2014). In addition to a range of shorter critical essays and articles, she edited *The Body: A Reader* (Palgrave, 2004). Before being appointed Professor in Creative Writing at the University of East Anglia, she lived in Aberystwyth, where she also lectured in the University.

I wanted to start by asking you about Catulla. She's terrific: where did she come from?
It was quite accidental, actually. I'd just heard C.K. Stead reading some of his Catullus poems at a festival and thought, I like this so much I want to read Catullus. So I did. And the character of Catulla came out of that. I don't think there's anything very original about the gender switch, but the tone, the ambivalence interested me a lot. Catullus is known chiefly for his excoriating attack poems but also those very plangent love poems. I wanted to bring together those two tones. It's usually quite playfully sincere, the lyric voice. But to get that kind of irreverence in the same voice seemed to me to be interesting.

You like irreverence; in fact you're very funny, you're good at humour...
Really? Thank you. I like it when people laugh at the poems. I have done readings in schools where the students feel they aren't supposed to find poetry funny, so I now make a point of telling them its okay to laugh, or groan, or whatever.

What was it like using a different language or were you happy to use translations?
Well approaching this obliquely as I did I didn't feel the need to be very strict. I am not pretending to be a classicist. There is already a terrific series of Catullus translations and 'updatings' by Josephine Balmer, who is one. Mine wasn't translation, more intervention or borrowing. I don't read Latin but I had English and Latin versions side by side. I studied the Latin poems, and what they looked like, how they were put together. I had several different translations: the ones which seem to strive most for linguistic accuracy are in blocks of prose. The more I found out about Latin forms and his interrogation of all kinds of forms, the more I came to admire Catullus. But when I started on mine I closed the books and just watched what came out.

Catulla herself is wonderfully achieved; she's a great read. And I hear him in her too, transformed but there. Was she fun to make?
Absolutely, yes. She's fickle and arsy and I like that about her but as a real person [*laughs*] I don't think she'd be terribly likeable. And to have a character with one foot in contemporary Wales and one foot in late Republican Rome. That interested me more than the gender switch actually.

It's quite an acrobatic feat to bring Wales and Italy into that kind of very close conjunction. How much farther could you get from Rome than Aberystwyth?
Well the maritime context is one of Catullus' contexts, of course, but I'm not sure that I was trying to suggest that there are similarities, I was just interested in the juxtaposition. It was more the sense of a community and a small world in which news travels fast, people know each other, people have little reputations. Catullus is very interested in that too, local reputations.

But he's cosmopolitan too. So I liked the comic value of mapping of smallish seaside town onto the more alien sophistications of an urban space; cramming Rome into Aber...
Yes I quite enjoyed the comical element in that. Catulla's

someone who kind of found herself washed up in this place. So maybe it's also that element of Aberystwyth; some people have arrived there from quite unconventional lives and so on: it's quite tolerant of that, of unconventional lifestyles. And it has its own set of 'mythic' places – the prom, the pier, certain pubs...

She seems both shallow and tortured, but she's also strong; she survives her mistakes. You're downplaying the gender switch, but you surely knew that these poems were saying things about women and poetry, in both timeframes. So how and why did you decide to make your speaker a woman?

The decision to have a female speaker was instant, and therefore hardly felt like a decision at all. And it didn't seem to present many immediate difficulties. A lot of the poems are about a frustrated erotic gaze and that seemed quite natural from the female viewpoint. One poem where it needed a bit more thought was '99' – after Catullus's poem 99 which is addressed to Juventius, a young boy, a catamite. I did wonder whether Catulla might address this homoerotically to a younger woman, or more heternormatively to a young man? It occurred to me that there aren't many poems by an older woman speaker to a much younger man, so I stuck with that.

Have you got a favourite poem in the sequence? And why?

I'm very fond of 'Hymen Hymeneus': it feels like a celebration, a mythification of my home town. And I enjoyed the patterning, and the blank stanza that I left blank (as in the damaged Catullus codex) because it is so beautifully suggestive. When I read the poem aloud I stay silent for the length of those empty lines.

The sequence as a whole seems to veer between sympathy for Catulla and almost prudish horror or at least disdain for her, in all her quirk-iness.

Well she seems to have a past, even if we don't learn much about it, but she also has all the pratfalls. There's a lot of embarrassment in that sequence. I'm interested in embarrassment and pratfalls and finding ways to frame them or hold them up to some kind of scrutiny. In my experience we live most of our lives like that. We don't have enormous revelations or I certainly don't; there are these little embarrassing revelations that happen through silly encounters, when you suddenly realize that you've been an idiot or when you try to do something that should go one way and doesn't. I like that.

Why does embarrassment interest you so much?
Well I find writing embarrassing. Particularly if you write lyric poetry (I'm not sure that I do) there's an assumption that you're revealing something about yourself. Perhaps you are, but I don't think it's ever a direct relationship. Being a woman and writing sometimes about sex and relationships and so forth, I've noticed that people find it embarrassing. It's not that they don't enjoy it or find it interesting, but then again maybe the lyric poem is at its best when it's embarrassing.

When it's dealing with embarrassing ideas?
Maybe, or simply when it's not seeking solace in form and irony and detachment. Whether it puts on an obvious mask or moves towards sincerity there's still the idea that it must reveal something about the self and that's embarrassing. Teaching writing is also embarrassing; workshops are embarrassing. And what we seem to do in the academy is try to teach people not to embarrass themselves. Maybe it's more interesting to take the risks of being more open, more exploratory, rather than learning from the start how to be detached and ironic.

It's not that writing offers a way out of (let's say gender-specific) embarrassment; a way to defuse or transform apparently embarrass-ing materials?
I don't think of it that way, though I suppose it could be a kind of metabolising of awkwardness! But you do have to assume that some people will take things you've written literally. And it seems to me that women take that risk more often and that their writing is more often referred to in those terms. But if there's something exposing about any kind of writing, even critical writing, it's out

of all proportion to the actual 'danger' of exposure. I mean hardly anyone reads poetry, still less academic books, really, do they?

I guess anyone publishes partly to expose their voice, in some way. Why else do it?
[*Laughing.*] Why do I do it? Because I'm curious about language, it gives me a thrill: it's some kind of compulsion. I don't think when I sit down to write: 'I am now going to tackle the lyric epiphany or worry about my voice'. It doesn't work that way. But the more you read and think the more likely you are to find the things you want to say or the things you want to rough up a bit. But I do like being published, so part of me must be seeking that exposure.

Have you always written?
No. I did a very conventional undergraduate degree at Birmingham from 1990 to 1993 and my MA and PhD – in critical theory – at Cardiff straight afterwards. Cardiff had a Creative Writing degree which was quite unusual then but that wasn't my degree. I wasn't really interested in writing myself until quite late, and then it was a kind of hobby, not what I thought of as part of a career or even subject of study.

So you began to write at university. You didn't write at school?
I wrote plays and things at school, never poetry. I started in my second or final year at university when there was a poet in the department, Steve Ellis, and he organised readings from contemporary poets like Simon Armitage, Selima Hill, Jo Shapcott and Anne Stevenson. And some of them were really young, and at the start of their careers, and it was tremendously exciting because we'd go from reading pre-Raphaelite poems, say, to Simon Armitage and it just blew me away.

So you went home and . . .
And had a go, yes. Really terrible formal poems – all sonnets – about things like snow. Utterly embarrassing. But I got one placed in a competition anthology, and started going to a

workshop group in Birmingham, and I just read a lot. I suddenly discovered that I wasn't frightened of contemporary poetry. So probably it was seeing those poets live. They looked like normal people. It sounds implausible now because curricula have changed a lot, but contemporary poetry just had not fallen across my path. So it was discovering this world that was in fact accessible.

In one of the essays you talk about the sheer bloody slog of it. Why the compulsion?
Utter pleasure. It was making something. At the time I was mostly studying philosophical theory. I was reading quite difficult theoretical texts and I really enjoyed that but it was breaking things down rather than making things. So writing was pleasurable time out.

Are you a maker in other ways? Do you make bread or patchwork quilts or anything?
I wish. I would love to be able to make stuff. I'd rather be musical, or be able to paint or something. Perhaps because it's more direct. More immediate. Even now music gets me faster than poetry. You have to work at poetry. But I love it. I love language. Just nailing something in language is really satisfying. The way language generates language. You can wind it up and let it go. The concentration; that I like. And it surprises you all the time. I never know what I'm going to end up with.

I was just thinking of the essay you wrote on the importance of difficulty? Isn't the reward of that 'nailing' of something in language commensurate with the effort?
Absolutely. And some kinds of reading, difficult reading, I think are valuable and pleasurable in a different way from the way we're usually taught to consume books; to read for content or instant message all the time. And I think we're missing a pleasure. There's a kind of voluptuousness about that kind of reading; you have to actively seek it out. I mean we're not generally presented with opportunities for that to happen but I think we

need them. It makes us more complex people. More at ease with, less intolerant of, complexity and ambivalence which seems a good thing.

Who might you turn to for that kind of writing?
Well that changes all the time, because I'm always trying to find new people but W.S. Graham is reliable. Jean Follain I've discovered reasonably recently in translation (Christopher Middleton's translations are really good). I was talking to Richard Gwyn about writers who make you want to write. And we agreed that Anne Carson's writing prompts the kind of reading which is most like writing. That's Richard's phrase, and I think it's really good. Alice Oswald. Always. There's something about her writing which sets me going again… every time. She's a very different kind of writer from me but it's something about the music of her writing, its kind of choric quality. Like Carson. They do things that you're not really supposed to be able to get away with just using language. It's like their work has a particular colour or tonal quality or maybe something more like a series of descending minor chords that is utterly distinctive. It's like they really work the language, bend it and hammer it until it almost becomes something else. Those possibilities are tremendously exciting and kind of sensuous.

The kinds of musical qualities you're describing are what I attribute to 'lyric' writing, the lyric poem. Yet you say you don't write lyric poetry and you're not musical…
I suppose what I have in mind by lyric may be a misuse of the term. I don't think of its musical pedigree when I use it as shorthand for a kind of sloppy confessionalism, which I'm trying to get away from, because I'm frightened of being accused of doing that.

Have you been accused of that?
Once or twice – about *Kink and Particle*.

I suppose that while I always know it's not you talking in Kink and

Particle, *it has a kind of unguarded quality which I don't hear as distinctly in* Catulla et al.

I think that's quite common for a first collection because it's often been written over the longest period, and includes early poems that maybe draw directly on personal experience. Or mine did as I didn't have the confidence to try anything else. So *Kink and Particle* includes poems which date from when I arrived in Aberystwyth. A lot of them are more closely related to actual things or people or feelings. I find that book quite embarrassing. But I realise I am being contradictory: speaking out for embarrassment when I don't want to feel embarrassed myself!

And that's not good?

[*Laughs.*] It depends which side of the embarrassment you're on doesn't it? Whether you're an embarrasser or an embarrassee, or just an onlooker. People recognised themselves in *Kink and Particle* though, and I am still mortified by that. I don't know why I didn't expect that to happen.

Was it that the mortification turned into Catulla?

I think that probably was the case. A fictionalising of scenarios so they have the same emotional freight but there is a little more distancing.

Catulla came out of Aberystwyth. I was wondering if she offered you a valve? A portal, even, a way out of Wales? Does she enable you to say things, perhaps in ways you otherwise wouldn't have?

Definitely. I think poems should always be places where you say things in ways that you wouldn't otherwise. Not in the sense of revealing personal secrets but in the way of using language differently, not as you do in everyday life. And yes there was a certain glee in that kind of attitude. Also the fun of sounding cosmopolitan when I am anything but...

She doesn't seem to care for Aber much. But you're fond of it?

Oh I'm so ambivalent about it. There's something very charming about it but it's a small town; it's where I've spent a large portion of my adult life but it does feel geographically remote.

Do you feel English there? You're not Welsh, and you've never pretended to be, but as a writer you've been grown in Wales.
My professional academic life has entirely been in Wales and I have a strong sense of affiliation with various Welsh issues but I do feel English, yes. But I'm army English, which means I don't think I'd feel at home or native anywhere. It's to do with never having lived anywhere for very long as a child or young person. Places all seem temporary to me. But I've been in Aberystwyth for 13 years. Well that's not temporary is it? I feel I belong just from the length of time I think. And I owe my entire writing life, apart from Steve Ellis's readings in Birmingham, to being in Wales.

Are you a traveller? If you could spirit yourself away where would you go?
Is this just for wellbeing and happiness? Or to do with writing? Because they're two different things I think.

That's interesting; writing isn't associated with happiness and wellbeing?
Ah yes but you are asking me on a cold November afternoon in Carmarthen! Right now I quite fancy a fortnight on a tropical beach... but yes, writing absolutely is wellbeing. And I don't think of places as being ones I can write in or not – everywhere is a place to write in – at the moment I would like people. Cities. Noise. New York! Berlin. Buenos Aires. Paris. Istanbul. I really crave that at the moment. And I think I would find that very kind of stimulating.

Are you a political person? Are you issue-driven?
That's really hard to answer. I recoil from slogans and manifestoes and easy soundbites. And unfortunately that seems the only way of being seen to be engaged with issues. But I mind about all kinds of exploitations and inequalities and manipulation of power and ways of somehow constraining other people's

freedoms. Freedom of expression, of feeling... And I mind very much about language. I get annoyed about commas in the wrong place and mixing up 'their' and 'there'. Because I think it's important to be precise. And it matters. Being able to articulate something, for yourself, well it's never ideal but it's all we've got. It's important to be particular and precise in everyday language or someone else will do your thinking for you, and probably very sloppily. I don't think you don't have to be a writer to care about that.

Can we talk about metaphor and precision? Because I'd say you sometimes use it to deflect rather than refine or sharpen an idea...
Well there are different ways of thinking about metaphor. It can clarify and make things more specific or equally it can multiply frames of reference and make things more mysterious and more numinous. In the past I've tended to use the former; I'm more and more interested in the latter. I think that's to do with tolerating or representing multiplicity and ambiguity. It's not really about irony, but trying to hold multiple layers in conversation with each other, like a palimpsest. Recognising and tolerating that uncertainty or ambivalence rather than brushing it away in a neat rhetorical flourish.

What's wrong with irony?
I'm a bit weary of irony as a trope or mode of writing. Maybe it's to do with the academy, you know, that 'we're too educated to be anything other than ironic' position. I get from that a sense that you can either be sincere or ironic, and that you're expected to 'mature' from one into the other. Baldly, I think it can become complacent. Although ironists probably intend to encourage thought it actually feels to me often as if it's an easy way out of thinking. Oh 'it's ironic...'; so okay, we don't have think about what was really meant there, what was smuggled in there. It's like a trump card. Somehow irony invites me to bypass a kind of thinking or emotional response – maybe that embarrasses or disturbs – in a way I've come to suspect. If we actually lived our lives with that much irony it wouldn't be much of a life and we

wouldn't really communicate. We would just trade in double-think. So I think it makes me a lazy reader; I've let someone else do doublethink for me. Grayson Perry said in one of his Reith Lectures that the really shocking, subversive thing these days is sincerity. You know even really assuming it were possible to be sincere – and we all know really that it isn't (which is an irony isn't it?) – we should still be trying a bit harder. [*Laughs.*] I think I should be trying a bit harder.

It sounds as if you'll never be satisfied by what you write. Are you good at knowing when you've finished? Do you put stuff down, or are you a tinkerer?
Well that's the nature of language isn't it? Form, matter. I like that. It's a creative dissatisfaction! I am a tinkerer, up to a point. The thing about poems, as opposed (I imagine) to a novel, is that you get lots of new starts, so you can give each your best shot then move on, try again.

Your new collection So Many Moving Parts *is about to appear. Can you tell me a bit about it?*
So Many Moving Parts was meant to be a nicely plotted series of poems about anatomy and bodies, along the lines of the theoretical materials I explored in my PhD. But as I find myself saying to students, poetry isn't criticism written backwards. When you set out to write the poems you have to be open to all kinds of unexpected directions. This happens in critical prose too of course, but the need for argument keeps you better tethered... Somehow it ended up being a collection of unflashy poems, quieter than the Catulla ones, and often observations of people and places. There's quite a lot of travelling but also some deliberately flatfooted moments. So, rather than trying to present some kind of epiphanic moment, to flesh out an idea, I began to introduce, say, an unanswerable question, or simply a flatfooted comment, like a stone in the shoe, an unexpected friction. It was something I noticed I was enjoying doing. That framing something in a little bubble was more interesting if it was a dented bubble. There's also quite a lot of patterning, repetition

and refrain, which I haven't really done much with before. That differentiates the poem from everyday utterance, makes it something stranger...

I'm intrigued. So the devices help to make the dents?
Yes, they are interruptions; little people from Porlock who puncture some kind of self-containment, maybe complacency. And repeated phrases and so on start to empty out their conventional referentiality and become a different way of creating meaning.

It sounds theatrical. In a sense pratfalls are theatre aren't they?
Well pratfalls are non-communication, non-verbal communication. They're not things that necessarily belong in poems. But if you can have linguistic ones, then yes.

Are pratfalls clowning – conscious – or more unfunny or accidental?
Well I don't think pratfalls and clowning are necessarily funny, though they are certainly embarrassing. But yes [*laughing*] there's endless embarrassment in bodies. In having a body.

You've written very interestingly on bodies in your critical anthology The Body Reader; *were bodies always an interest?*
There's a sort of standard feminist response to that isn't there? In that women experience their bodies so powerfully from puberty onwards that it's difficult to imagine otherwise. I wasn't aware of being particularly interested in them. It was body theory and feminist theory which switched me on to them as a subject of enquiry in their own right. My PhD was called 'The Dissenting Flesh: Corporeality, Representation and Theory'. This was the heyday of crazy theory and people were publishing papers on the semantics of Derrida's ashtray and what-have-you. The body stuff was still new and it fascinated me that you could apply theory to this stuff that you're walking around in, reading in, kissing in, shitting in, etc. It was really radical for me. I was particularly interested in psychoanalysis, the drama of bodies, and the history of anatomy: how we come to think of ourselves

as bounded individuals, envelopes of contents, psychic contents, intellectual contents, emotional and, of course, visceral ones. There was quite a lot on the history of art and representation and how the surface signifies. I brought some fairly far out critical theory to bear on embodiment, but the bodies always upstage the theory by being weirder and more complex. Thrilling, then. Now bodies and theory have become more familiar.

You've written on the celebrity anatomist and plastinator of 'Body Worlds' fame Gunther Von Hagens
I was intrigued by him. I may write more – critically – about that; creatively I don't know. Over-thinking something from a critical perspective can make it a bit of a dead end creatively (as it were). I first encountered Von Hagens in the first UK exhibition in Brick Lane in 2001 and it was really new. Now it's not. So the contexts of consuming those bodies are changing all the time; they've become part of the cultural imagination, which has already changed something about how we think of ourselves, our mortality, about how we perceive health and illness and how we look at other people's bodies. Of course the main thing about being in a body is suffering, isn't it? That's something else I was interested in.

But we can't learn much from those exhibitions about suffering can we, or language?
I think it would have been intolerable if those exhibitions had tackled pain but they had nothing to do with it. And yes the rubric of the exhibitions I've seen has always been quite banal: look how magnificent our bodies are – so quit smoking and get more exercise. Someone should commission some creative writers to respond to the next one.

Embarrassment is pain isn't it? Social pain.
It's extraordinary how we try to avoid embarrassment as if it might actually damage you. And it's momentary. I think I spend more of my life trying to avoid embarrassment than actual physical harm. Which seems so craven, so norm-bound in the most superficial way. What kind of pain is social pain? It ought to be

negligible, but it doesn't feel so. What is that telling us about the constraints we place around communication and tolerance? Not good things I suspect. Writing is a way of getting all this up front. I deliberately switch off my embarrassometer when I'm writing…

Your writing often conjures the poem as a kind of body. Catulla's genuinely interested in her own and other people's bodies. The way they look, the way they touch and are touched.
She's very observant. And there's a lot of observation in *So Many Moving Parts*; a lot about bodies and hands and touching

Why hands? Because they're important to talking?
And to writing. It's quite difficult to find a page of prose without a hand in it. You can't write about people without referring to hands. They're prime signifiers. I love hands. I can't explain it. There are just certain things or words which have idiosyncratic magical power. Hands do that for me.

Do you think language has magical power?
No but I think it can feel damn close to it. Things happen to me through other people's writing; reading can just change everything in your head. It's not magic but nor can you explain those neural connections or mechanisms or whatever; it's just incredibly powerful.

More than the sum of its parts.
Yes. That's another thing about *So Many Moving Parts*. That language is exactly that; in that overused phrase of the American poet William Carlos Williams, it's 'a machine made of words'. Obviously language is working parts, moving in both senses. I like this idea because it removes a bit of self from the equation; allows language to do its own thing while you push it around. Like a Hoover – I don't really understand how all the parts work but I like pushing it around.

I love that image. Thank you Tiffany.

RUTH BIDGOOD

Ruth Bidgood has produced thirteen full collections including four selected volumes: *The Given Time* (Christopher Davies, 1972); *Not Without Homage* (Christopher Davies, 1975); *The Print of Miracle* (Gomer, 1978); *Lighting Candles: New and Selected Poems* (Poetry Wales Press, 1982); *Kindred* (Poetry Wales Press, 1986); *Selected Poems* (Poetry Wales Press, 1992); *The Fluent Moment* (Seren, 1996); *Singing to Wolves* (Seren, 2000); *New and Selected Poems* (Seren, 2004); *Symbols of Plenty: Selected Longer Poems* (Canterbury Press, 2006); *Hearing Voices* (Cinnamon, 2008), *Time Being* (Seren, 2009); and *Above the Forests* (Cinnamon, 2012). She is also the author of numerous articles and several longer works of local history focussing on the environs of Abergwesyn (Powys), the most substantial of which is *Parishes of the Buzzard* (Gold Leaf, 2000). She lives near Llanwrtyd Wells.

Could we begin with some biography? I know you worked in London after coding in Egypt during the war. Coding sounds rather glamorous. What came next?
Oh coding was quite humble! You just put signals in plain language into code or decoded them out of code into plain language. Although I hadn't any qualifications to follow my English degree I managed to get a job with *Chambers Encyclopedia* for a while after the war. I got married in December 1946 and moved to Coulsdon, five miles south of Croydon, where we lived for the next twenty years. And eventually with a small legacy we bought the house in mid-Wales.

And had three children. Did you carry on working?
No, I was at home, which was the norm. In our road, which had
quite a feel of a little community about it, there were only about
two women who worked outside the home.

Did you miss Oxford?
I missed Oxford. I loved it: I didn't realise how hard it was to get
there and how lucky I had been to get there. But I made some
effort to break away from all that side of my life, really. I felt you
had three years there and then it was over. At one point I burnt
all my essays and the things that I'd saved up: I believed I should
cut off the past. I don't think that now. Getting fascinated by
Abergwesyn, feeling layers of time and their richness and excitement, changed my attitude. I have more sense now of the unity
of time, and its non-linear nature.

*Living in Coulsdon, raising your children, you weren't yearning after
books? Were you writing?*
I was leading a pretty brainless life really. I tried to write short
stories which is peculiar because I'm rather ignorant about short
story-writing. I think the thought of writing long fiction rather
appalled me. I liked reading it; I liked a novel to make a world that
I could walk about in, but I didn't think I could make a world like
that for readers.

But you were still reading; you weren't shunning that part of you?
I don't think I was shunning it but I wasn't really feeding it very
thoroughly. And my husband was a scientist. The only one of the
arts that he really cared about was music.

He wasn't Welsh?
He was partly Welsh, like me, but had gone to school in England
and then to Cambridge. But I was more bonded to Wales than he
was, and eventually that proved divisive.

How did you find the cottage? Why Abergwesyn?
We'd really been looking for a traditional Welsh stone cottage in

Radnorshire, which is the county next door to North Breconshire, where we'd had two holidays. We hadn't managed to find one and then an agent in Builth said, 'I have a little corrugated iron bungalow which looks much prettier than it sounds up what I think is the most wonderful valley in mid-Wales; would you like to see it?' Well by the time we were halfway up the valley we really had fallen in love with the area. I certainly had.

And how much time did you spend here in the first ten years?
All the holidays. My youngest one Martin was nine. He was the one who put down his roots here. Tony, the elder one, was at the time more rootless. Janet my daughter is dead but she spent some of her happiest days here. She was very keen on horses, and the farmers would lend her horses to ride.

Had you started writing before you found the cottage?
No. We bought the house in 1964, came on the first holiday in 1965 and by 1966 I was starting to have one or two poems published. The first poem got accepted by *Country Life*. It was a great day when I had a poem accepted by *Poetry Wales*. And I started to read magazines, especially the *London Welshman*, and magazines published in Wales, to find out who was doing what. I still do.

Were you reading poetry before then?
Not a lot. But then I started reading poems again more when I came back to Wales. Everything seemed to wake up.

Can you think of any poets you were reading when you started writing perhaps? Do you remember trying to copy other writers?
I read a lot of poetry at Oxford, although the syllabus ended at 1830. Of course I read outside it too. I loved Donne. I still do. But I don't think I practised in any deliberate way. Edward Thomas was about the only influence I'm clear about. I read him while I was at Oxford (not for the syllabus) and started re-reading him when somebody lent me a little selection of his poems. It was like coming into a house you recognise but don't remember being in

before. And then two people, one was Jeremy Hooker, said that I
had learned from R.S.Thomas how to structure a verse
paragraph. I seem to tend to write in paragraphs of free-verse,
although I prefer the term 'conversational': 'free' sounds a bit
sloppy.

Did it take a lot of courage to start sending the poems off?
No. It seemed the obvious thing to do, to try. I was more prolific
when I first started writing than now; I was writing perhaps two
poems a week. I think the first one to be published was called
'Llanddewi Hall, Radnorshire'. I wrote it when the whole family
was sitting round watching the World Cup!

Your interest in old houses goes right back, as The Given Time
proves.
I suppose it's a kind of vessel for life really. I love life, and people,
but I also love off-beat things. Perhaps it's something to do with
not liking cut-and-dried explanations. I like the things that slide
in at the edge of the mind, or have a significance I don't fully
understand. In one or two poems I mention that a ruined house,
one which is very ruined indeed, is like the beginning of a house.
I suppose I feel it's a cyclical thing, leaving and returning . . .

When did you find your first ruined house?
When I went to Abergwesyn. They're all over the place. Up the
valley, there are clusters of them. They were quite solitary houses
really, but there were several of them in each valley, forming a
little community.

*So it's as much the community as the house; it's partly about that
larger cultural context?*
Yes. The houses you might assume were terribly lonely weren't
necessarily. I talked to a woman who'd been brought up in the
Tywi valley where the farms, now ruins, were always scattered,
and she said it wasn't a lonely life. The houses were full because
the families were large, and the bigger farms had lots of young
servants, and in the evenings they'd ride about on ponies from

house to house and play cards and sing. It was very friendly.

But for some people it was lonely. The postlady who lived next door – here, in Beulah – had a bike and used to go up the valleys round here. She'd be the only person the wife up there had seen for days. He'd be out shepherding or gone to market, and she'd be totally alone in a very isolated house so the postlady was company. And another woman, that counted too.

You settled here after your divorce.
Yes. I moved into Abergwesyn in 1974, after ten years of coming for holidays, so I was there quite a long time on my own. At first my younger son was coming and going. Apart from that I was living on my own, but much visited by friends.

So, being on your own, did you identify with those kinds of fragmented existences?
I don't think I identified with them. I've never deluded myself that I was one of the local farming community. But I always got on with the farmers; we led parallel but friendly lives, and I was always interested in all parts of the life.

You've quoted Harri Webb's description of this area as 'a hole in the heart of Wales.' What do you mean?
Well a hole in the heart is an illness; I don't look upon mid-Wales as a sickness in Wales. But I do think of this as a kind of enclosed part of Wales, perhaps womb-like or shell-like. That's why I get distressed when the area's wilderness is threatened. I think we need our wildernesses. There were plans for a huge windfarm between here and Tregaron on the Cambrian Mountains. And the pipeline, which runs near the house of a friend in Myddfai near Llandovery, also caused a lot of objections although the landscaping process seems to have left people happier about it.

You've always been protective of this area; I'm thinking of the Forestry Commission.
Yes. My son says I've been hard on the Forestry. I suppose it has been protective in some ways; planting and planning are much

more sensitive nowadays, and once their roads started getting a bit decrepit they became rather beautiful. There's one glade in the forests on the western bank of the Tywi: up an old track to a ruined farm. There's a fantastically beautiful little glade there, with mosses I haven't seen anywhere else. So I forgive them in a limited way. And having grandchildren growing up with the forest, having happy associations with them, has softened my attitude.

What do you not forgive?
Excessive encroachment in some areas. Round here we got a very big dose of Forestry. If you look east towards Abergwesyn from across the Tywi, standing on the other bank, you see darkness over all the hills; a mat of dark. The planting's started to get better, but it used to be just serried ranks of spruce, in very rulered lines down the hill, bisected by the Forestry roads. Unlike the Brecon Beacons and other well-known beauty spots this is neither a National Park nor, officially, an 'area of outstanding natural beauty' (though it is just that). So it's very vulnerable, very unprotected. Four-wheel drive vehicles and powerful bikes churn up the old hill tracks and open moors of our mountain countryside, destroying our silence – one of our most valued assets. But I also care for what is still alive. I don't want the living farms to go, because you've got to have some of the land being worked. You've got to find a balance: if you cut out the wild you impoverish human life.

You've written about the gradual disappearance of the working farms in 'All Souls' (The Print of Miracle).
If light shines from a house, there's life in it. Like other hill areas, Abergwesyn has lost many working farms and occupied cottages which once would have sent out their lights, however dim in the pre-electricity days. Now they are dark. In 'All Souls' I imagine the few remaining lit houses as having to shine (speak) for ones where light shines no longer.

I've noticed how often your poems return to the subject of darkness and light.

I'm not sure at what point the imagery of dark and light started to be so important to me. Possibly not before Abergwesyn and the experience of living in a remote countryside where night is deeply dark, and the lights of scattered houses and an occasional car become very significant in marking the presence of human life. It's not always 'light good, dark bad', of course. Light can be hurtful glare; dark can be gentle: the acceptance of mystery. Mostly, light combined with the image of the house clearly connects it with life, although in 'Omen' (*New and Selected Poems*) the procession of lights means marks the route of the future funeral procession, and in 'Strangeness' (*The Fluent Moment*) the ruined house offers up its 'votive candle of dark'. I hope that the uncertainty remains fertile.

'All Souls' raises some of the same ideas as 'Valley before Night' (Selected Poems). *In that poem, villagers seem to try to hold the darkness – or something similar, disturbing – at bay in the unusual practice which the poem describes,* dechreunos. *No-one I've asked knows much about it. Was it particular to this area?*
I think it might have been. I was told about it by two great friends of mine, who lived at Abergwesyn post office and shop, Dai and Thirza Jones. A poem by T. Harri Jones, the Llanafan (North Breconshire) poet, mentions the 'grudged candlelight'. The candlelight was grudged because it was a terrible job in the autumn making the candles to last through the winter. Once you'd got them you wanted them to last. In this area there was a custom that in each valley, every evening, most people wouldn't light up their houses at all: they'd simply bank the fire up and meet at one house, which would light all of its candles. This was *dechreunos*.

Every single night?
I couldn't swear that I understood it properly but I think it was every night. They took turns. They'd gather for a few hours to chat, enjoying the light and then go back to their own homes for their bowl of cawl, or whatever, stoke the fire for a bit of light to avoid lighting their own candles, and go to bed early.

Can you tell me about the Valley and how that poem came about?
That valley runs parallel with the Cnyffiad valley that goes down
from Abergwesyn to Beulah. That's the one with the road in it;
there's a hill on the left going downstream with a pass going over.
This drops down the other side into the Camarch valley, which
has never had a motor road in it: it never had any road beyond
farm tracks until the Forestry came. One day I walked up behind
Pantycelyn chapel to the pass and looked down into the Camarch
valley and it seemed terribly remote and weird. I thought it was
creepy but in a way that intrigued rather than put me off. And
then I started hearing the stories. That the name of it in Welsh
was *Cwm-cyn-nos*, or 'valley-before-night' and meant that you
mustn't hang about with night coming on. You had to get home
or get out of the valley; not wander about in it. I wondered about
the *dechreunos* and whether the people heading to the one house
would admit to feeling creepy about the journey.

And your grandchildren lived there.
Martin's children lived a little bit lower down. They were the only
children actually growing up in that valley. But the whole valley
is absolutely magical. I dearly loved their home there,
Coedtrefan. I think the poem shows my fascination and involvement with that valley, especially as a family home.

*Does that mysterious 'air' of the valley seem intrinsic to you? Or do
you think of it as having been somehow engendered, perhaps by the
people there; as a kind of cultural legacy?*
I really don't know what influences what... I find the atmosphere
of places, the power that one feels in some places, very intriguing
and hard to understand. Sometimes it can appear benign,
sometimes quite the reverse. Very often it's neutral, like the poem
I wrote about the Green Man (*Selected Poems*). He could be
either, really.

*I'm interested in how and why you transfer those atmospheres into the
frame of the poem. You've called yourself a remembrancer.*
I think a 'remembrancer' traditionally would be somebody who

was conscious of the fact that they were trying to save the past in the present, who was trying to keep in the present what was valuable about the past. I think with the Camarch valley I felt that something valuable had gone, that these were places where real farm life and community had gone, and that I wanted in the poem to keep that.

So the poem is a kind of memorial? Or a talisman? I wondered if it implied that the valley had somehow got the better of it?
I rarely have a specific intention: I respond to what seems to claim my attention. The stories of that valley are not benign. It's felt to be a dark valley as the man says in the poem. But I'm often neutral; more of a reporter. Though that wouldn't account for my *love* of the place.

You said to me earlier that you had a lot of fun writing that poem.
I liked the technical problems. For instance the poem about Gwyn is quite a light-hearted poem. He seemed to be a very carefree sort of baby, or he is in the poem, and I didn't want anything too dark next to him, to weigh him down too much. I enjoyed wondering where to slot in the little local traditions, the tombstone section, for example. That kind of decision.

Did you set out to write a sequence?
I think of it as a long poem. Sometimes people ask me to read from 'Valley Before Night' and I always say, I can't read *a bit* of it: it's all one. Various elements dovetail into each other but it isn't a chain of poems like my sequences.

How do you decide which suits which subject?
I don't know. Some sequences start with one or two poems written separately and then I see they'd be better together and better still with something else alongside. Some are sequences from the beginning. 'Into the Dark' was always a sequence. I think on the whole you write a sequence to treat different aspects of a theme. They could be clustered together or distinct but they'll share a link at the core. I love to work in sequences. Once

you've started, it's a great incentive to have to find the next little building block. But yes, when you write a poem as part of a sequence, you are stressing that part of your subject which relates to the theme of the sequence, and down-playing other connections. You're not so much escaping as seeking artistic unity.

You're doing more and more sequences. My favourite is 'Singing to Wolves', partly because you seem to be writing about your art. Do you feel a sense of responsibility to your profession, to your culture, even?
I feel very privileged to be able ever to write a poem that passes muster at all. I think it's an honour to have the most small gift in that line. It's a wonderful feeling.

Is it scary? Do you think of the poem as having a power which is not yours?
Oh yes, I think of a poem as having a power which is not yours, and I think the business of the *awen* or the inspiration is very peculiar. It seems to be a combination of something that seems to come from outside and something that comes from deep within you.

Can we turn to another sequence? 'Guérinou' seems to me not unlike 'Valley Before Night'.
It's another dark one. Raymond Williams said it was the old name for an area of the Black Mountains which includes the Grwyne Fawr and Grwyne Fechan valleys. I don't know it well but I'm very drawn to it. The valleys are both beautiful, but very different. Grwyne Fechan is benign, it seems to me, and Grwyne Fawr rather malign. The contrast – so unexpected – fascinates me. Perhaps there's a sound practical reason, say in their geology, but that doesn't eliminate the frisson. I got very interested in the house, the Hermitage, a rather stately ruin, and the lady whom nobody knows anything about. There's no proof she existed, just a very strong tradition that John McNamara of Llangoed – now a posh hotel on the way down the Wye valley – kept a mistress in the Grwyne Fechan valley and used to ride over one of the high passes of the mountain to visit her. And I imagined her snowed-

up there. If you don't actually know anything you can imagine what you like. I imagined her as vulnerable, and very dominated by him but besotted and very jealous of his wife (who was a wonderful manager and more or less ran the estate, and their high-society life in London). I think the girl at the Hermitage would very likely have taken to the bottle; alone except for perhaps a servant or two, the snow coming down and her man at home with his wife.

I'm interested in your use of poems to remember Mid-Walian culture, the Wales you are writing from. How did the interest in local history start?
It happened at exactly the same time as I started to write the poems; it was the same stimulus. Walking, seeing things, photographing them, wondering about the life they meant. My (local) son always asks why I stick with the gentry in the local history articles. Well they had these interesting little-known houses, and you can find out a lot about them in the deeds. People living in a cottage can be hell to find out anything about. You can track the minor gentry down. But in my book about Abergwesyn most of it is not about the gentry at all and nor are many of my poems.

Are you aware of being particularly drawn to the part women played in that history, in remembering it from their angle?
A number of my poems are about men too, even monologues; I'm not overly conscious of wanting to construct a gendered version of a story. I suppose I get grabbed by certain personalities and situations. Some of these are women, several of them in some sort of crisis moment; facing bereavement and the threat of their own death ('Omen') for instance.

Would it seem better to talk about 'the woman in Wales', or 'the Welsh woman', so that it became a cultural rather than a gender issue?
Probably yes. The ones I have figured in my poems have either been Welsh women or women in a Welsh situation. But I always think, stick to the structure, that's what you need, that's what matters, that's what you've got. No need to imagine anything

else. That's why I'm so interested in what's left; what I can see and touch now. And how often that's been where the imagining has started!

Yes – you imagine the abandoned 'Shepherd's Cottage' (The Given Time), for example, to the point of filling it with people.
In fact I didn't have much imagining to do in that instance because that was my friend Dai's childhood home. He told me about how his sister and his brother and he used to sleep up in the loft and go up the ladder into the loft.

But that poem's also making, or remaking, that culture. Constructing more than remembering?
Yes I think it is. You make, and what you make isn't just repeating what you've been told. You add the elements which are part of your own response, inevitably coloured by your feeling about what you've been told.

Do you think being a woman has made a difference to your writing, the poems you've chosen to make?
Not really. Because my experience has not been of feeling put down because I was a woman, or of being unpublished because I was a woman. So gender has never been forced into my consciousness. When I first sent poems off to a publisher, I was certainly diffident. I didn't at all assume they'd be accepted. But the fact that they might not have been accepted because I was a woman never entered my head. That's been hard for some people to understand. Gillian Clarke once introduced a reading of mine at a dinner and she said something about a poem of mine giving her courage to write herself, as I was a woman living in Wales. I never had that anxiety!

Did you, do you consciously hunt out the work of other women? Say, Sylvia Plath?
I neither hunt them out nor avoid them. Sylvia Plath I could admire but not love. As a friend put it, she was brilliant but not nourishing. I remember feeling that, while feeling intensely sorry

for her at the same time. I felt I really wouldn't have liked her as a person, but I think her poems are brilliant. A lot of poets whose work I enjoy are women writing in Wales. I admire Gillian [Clarke]; I have all her books. I really love some of her poems. I remember the first poem that really resonated with me was 'The Sundial'. That spoke to me very much. I'm not spoken to quite so much by folding sheets and light shining through marmalade. I've folded sheets and made marmalade but I don't feel an urge to write poems about them, which she can do very beautifully. I like many of Sheenagh Pugh's poems; some of them are very moving. I am particularly fond of her early sequence 'Earth Studies'. I increasingly admire and enjoy Anne Cluysenaar – she achieves a wonderful mix of simplicity and profundity. But R.S. Thomas and John Burnside, along with Donne and Edward Thomas, remain my absolute favourite poets.

'The Sundial' takes us back to light and darkness. Or, perhaps shadows. You seem always drawn to that tension between light and the dark.
Yes, perhaps it's shadows. They're ambivalent, aren't they; they can caress or menace. Again, I think that's about the uncertainty out of which I write. Living in mid-Wales with a North Welsh father and born and brought up in South Wales, and now living in mid-Wales – and of course having a West Country mother, with Cornish ancestry – uncertainty is surely a natural outcome? In my poem 'Pathetic Fallacy' (*The Fluent Moment*) I call it 'fertile uncertainty'.

How and why 'fertile'? Is certainty somehow sterile?
I think I find certainty confining. For example, the question of whether I am a religious poet or not. I wouldn't say I've no religious dimension to my life but I don't like things to be cut and dried. For me religion, sciences and the arts all probe a mystery. So I prefer the end of a poem to start something, really. I like to think of the end of a poem as the beginning of something.

Uncertainty brings me back to mid-Wales. I've been trying to work out exactly where it is. Where its edges are. Do you think of mid-Wales as having edges and if so where are they, for you?

When I leave Powys, I feel that's a boundary really, crossing from Powys into Carmarthenshire, which properly counts as West Wales. The other way, I always feel Montgomeryshire lines up more with North Wales but then it's part of the *county* of Powys, whose boundaries don't match those of the (more northern) ancient territory called Powys. Borderlands – I'm thinking especially of Powys' eastern borders – seem to have a special sort of inspiration in them, perhaps because they bring diverse things together. As indeed poetry does.

Am I right in thinking that Strata Florida is (still) some kind of centre, although perhaps not geographically?

Yes Strata Florida is still very important hereabouts. When we first came here the old people like Dai still used it as for directions. If you asked how far somewhere was they'd say, well it's eight miles from here to the Abbey and then from there... For them, all those centuries on from when Abergwesyn was Strata Florida's grazing land, the Abbey was still a presence. It had been a centre for charity, hospitality and education. But then the Cistercians were more accepted in Wales than other orders because they were good sheep-farmers and very practical. Their simplicity and austerity suited the bare hills and the hard life.

I think of you as being more interested in Wales than Welshness really. But you often use Welsh words and Welsh names, so I'm guessing you know how to say them...

That's all my father taught me to do. Instead of bringing me up bilingual he taught me to pronounce the Welsh. I can't understand why I didn't question that, now. I didn't unquestioningly accept what my parents said or did – but I didn't see the strangeness of this compromise until I was adult. My father lived in South Wales most of his life, so didn't sound like a North Welshman. His Welsh accent was southern. I don't know enough Welsh to know whether, when he spoke Welsh, he'd have used North Welsh vocabulary. I imagine it was probably more South Welsh.

Who would you say you're writing for, do you think? Someone who is or thinks of themselves as being Welsh?
I think I'm always talking to somebody, communicating. I don't know who [*laughs*]; they could come from absolutely anywhere. I don't feel I'm just expressing myself; I hope my poems talk to anyone who wants to listen.

Sometimes the 'I' suggests that a poem draws on your own experiences ('Strata Florida' is one). Sometimes there's a 'she' who's plainly not you. Does knowing when it is and isn't you matter?
I don't think it does much. I don't think I use autobiography in that way. Sometimes it coincides. There's a poem in my first book called 'Storm' which seems very autobiographical but wasn't at all. It's a very unhappy poem, with a kite which comes to symbolize loneliness. I wrote it when I really wasn't unhappy in my life; I just saw the symbolism. I think people don't realise the importance of technicalities in writing. You feel things like anybody, but because you're a poet you notice that you can use things. I suppose I'm not a confessional poet, even if my poems are full of my life and feelings. Just not literally.

Looking at your recent collections – Time Being *and* Above the Forests *– do you sense anything about your writing nowadays, about your mature voice?*
Perhaps my themes have grown more varied, despite, as the title of *Above the Forests* signals, my continuing bond with Abergwesyn. It also spells out my changed attitude to those forests. I think that place and personal emotion may be more obviously interwined in my latest books.

You've talked about poetry making patterns where there aren't any, but you're so often drawn to the strangeness and beauty of not knowing, of having to guess the mystery. That equally sits uneasily with the puzzle-solving of local history. Does the poet take over when the facts run out?
I like the two different disciplines. In local history you sometimes can't find many facts; you've got to stick with what you've got,

however meagre. You can say something seems likely but remains unproven. With a poem, it's a virtue to imagine, not something you have to own up to! I doubt whether one sort of writing affects the other, apart from sometimes perhaps an overlap of subject matter... I am a bit irritated when people think they've found biographical bits in something I've invented or greatly modified. There's always more in a poem than you might think.

So your claim that poetry makes patterns begins to sound a bit disin-genuous –
Yes. Poetry does make patterns, it shapes the stuff it works with, but the patterns change and shift and vary. As I've said, the end of a poem can be a beginning for the reader who's willing to 'go with the flow'...

So the poems reach out of their patterns?
Yes. I feel they go on from there. I hope they go on from there.

Thank you very much.

ANNE CLUYSENAAR

Anne Cluysenaar has published seven volumes of poetry: *Nodes: Selected Poems 1960-1968* (Poetry Ireland Editions/Dolmen Press, 1971); *Double Helix* (Carcanet, 1982); *Timeslips: New and Selected Poems* (Carcanet, 1997); *Batu-Angas: Envisioning Nature with Alfred Russel Wallace* (Seren, 2008); *Water to Breathe* (Flarestack Poets, 2009); *Migrations* (Cinnamon, 2011) and *Touching Distances* (Cinnamon, 2014). She worked in higher education for many years, has authored articles and several scholarly works on language and linguistics, has produced critical editions of the works of Henry Vaughan and James Burns Singer, and co-edited anthologies of poetry. She helped found and was the first editor of *Scintilla*, the yearly journal of the Vaughan Association and acted as poetry editor for issues 1-15.[1]

Can we start by talking about your interest in natural history? It's perhaps most obvious in Batu-Angas, *the collection you wrote about the great naturalist Alfred Russel Wallace, but it runs throughout your work, really.*

I've been interested in nature and natural history all my life. I remember one of the first books that really impressed me was by Ernest Thompson Seton. I think it was called *Wild Animals I Have Known*, and it had little pawprints along the side of the text; I thought they were real ones (laughs). I like thinking about how things behave, and how they work in relation to each other. I wonder where humanity's place is, and where we all are in terms of evolution and extinction.

Can you tell me a bit more about what you mean?
Well let's take one of my favourite writers – Henry Vaughan, the subject of my 'Vaughan Variations' (*Timeslips*). Vaughan's experiential approach to religion is fascinating. There's a passage in 'Vanity of Spirit' where, after a night literally 'spent' in thought, he walks to the little spring on the hillside behind his farm. He recalls how he's analysed nature, looking for the source or 'spring' of creation, without success, until he came to 'traces and sounds of a strange kind' in himself, which seemed to be part of 'this mighty spring'. That poem seems to favour inner experience over analytical reasoning. Despite Vaughan's commitment to Christian doctrine, you can hear Keats' 'negative capability' very clearly in the pursuit of what Keats famously calls 'uncertainties, mysteries, doubts, without any irritable reaching after fact and reason'. We understand so much now about what that poem calls 'the Creatures' and 'the spheres', but knowledge always leaves gaps for the imagination.

How did you find your way to Wallace?
It started with natural history trips with Colin Titcombe, an expert on this region. When we stopped across the bridge from Usk, Colin pointed out a little house under the hill as the birthplace of Alfred Russel Wallace. I remembered the magical bird of paradise named after Wallace and it went from there.

Your poems explore Wallace through his collections, his specimens, and of course your friend the poet Graham Hartill has described one of your poems as a 'specimen'.
Reading Wallace's autobiography made me want to explore nature through his life and work. I'd have loved to spend time in the Malay Archipelago or the Amazon, to see what led him into it. I've a different kind of mind: I'd never discover anything left to myself. And I find it hard to kill things; I'm very amazed by life, by things existing. But I couldn't afford the trips, so I visited the specimens and imagined him handling them. Why did he nearly faint, handling a new butterfly when he caught it that first time? I can feel astonished watching a midge hesitate, as if it's thinking,

on the edge of my page when I'm reading out of doors (I try to read and write out of doors as much as I can).

Using words to explore those tiny details also distances them, of course.
Yes. My new collection, which is called *Touching Distances*, includes these lines about a caterpillar: 'He can't know the world, only be in it.... / A twig of life. Not made by itself. / Knowing how to wait and wait and wait.'

All you can do is put one word after another. And even when you've put words around it, you haven't got it really. I always think of what Gwyn Williams says of old Welsh poets and poetry in *The Burning Tree* (1979). He says they [reading] 'were not trying to write poems that would read like Greek temples or even Gothic cathedrals but, rather, like stone circles or the contour-following rings of the forts from which they fought, with hidden ways slipping from one ring to another.'

In your edition of his Selected Poems, *you quote James Burns Singer calling a poem a riddle without the answers.*
That's a good way of thinking about it. Singer also says 'thought is always and only thought: / The thinking's different: Thinking's in the blood'.

I very much liked being able to hear Wallace's own voice in Batu-Angas.
Yes I really wanted him to be in it because Wallace has given me so much. That's why I wanted the royalties to go to the World Wildlife Fund. Take the image of the bird of paradise which we reproduced on the front of the collection. Wallace describes seeing a sort of violet shimmer on the top of the head when he was handling that specimen. When I looked at the bird-skins which you can visit in the Natural History Museum at Tring (in Hertfordshire), I'd forgotten about that description, until suddenly I saw that violet shimmer on the top of the head and realised I'd got it at exactly the angle Wallace himself must have held it at. There's something fascinating about crossing that

boundary between oneself and another human being. And
another time. For me writing is a way of doing that; leaving a life
to be shared, if somebody wants to share it. I wanted to explore
that in my sequence 'Clay' (*Migrations*), the attempt to make
contact with a distant poetic and spiritual past.

*Wallace seems more mentor than influence. Do you think you'd have
liked him?*
I think so. He was extraordinarily open-minded. He really
respected women. He realised that people develop partly because
of the culture that they're in. That made him a socialist, and
respectful towards other people and cultures. He seems to have
been more open-minded than Darwin, who was of course his
contemporary: he was able to value how other people saw things
even if that differed from how he saw things. He could switch
cultural languages. He could be shy in company but I've often
thought I'd find him easy to talk to. If you said something he
didn't agree with, he would talk with you about it.

*I thought of the poems as dialogue. Simultaneously, with Wallace
himself, with the curators or guides who show you the specimens, and
also carrying on a conversation with you and your own 'art' –*
Dialogue, yes. And coming to terms with what, in one of the
poems, I call 'the tenuous job of poet'... Perhaps as a poet today
you can feel threatened by scientists who are really 'finding out
things'. Are we finding out anything?

Do you feel you are? What?
Maybe that's where Vaughan and Wallace come together. For
self-aware creatures like us, inner life – holding one's balance
there – is related to survival. Language may have had evolutionary roles to play since prehistory. Precision has something to do
with it. Take the *longimanus* beetle, with its great long arms. Take
the curator George Beccaloni, who worked on Wallace's collections; I think of him, tracing Wallace's note about the specimen's
size, realising that Wallace had had the beetle reproduced in its
actual size.[2] And Wallace's grandson Richard, selling his farm,

coming upon the boxes – full of bits – in the loft and deciding to ring George. George taking them home; restoring them took him hours and hours, but the specimens look wonderful now, pristine. I tried to be equally precise, about what Wallace and the artist and George did, and about the beetle, and about what it means to me, to imagine that I'm seeing the beetle fully, as Wallace must have seen it when he saw it. To somehow get into words what it means to us, as human beings, to see: to reverence reality, life, and experience, whatever mysteries are still out of sight.

It's the whole: beetle, scrutiny, illustration, reconstructed beetle.
The drawing is astoundingly precise. When you look at the beetle's carapace, you realise that one part is crenellated all the way along its edge and another is absolutely smooth. It's in the drawing; tiny but there. That draughtsman was devoted to getting it right, and making a nice picture as well. Likewise I've got to feel that what I make is a poem. The style of the sequence emerged poem by poem as it went along. I didn't plan it, beyond wanting to include Wallace's prose. I needed a kind of verse-line that wouldn't crack if you put prose into it. I only gradually realised that I was writing about poetry as well.

Back to art. Why do we use art to express ourselves do you think?
There's a kind of art-shaped space in modern culture; but do we really need it? Is it just a cultural leftover or is it of evolutionary value? I think it is. It goes back to the Neanderthals leaving amber and flowers where they buried their dead. Sparing time for that and, later, for cave art; it must have had importance. I'm not very concerned with literary fashion because I would like my writing to be still in some way valid in a thousand years, if it's there and there's anyone to read it. And you have to be what you are; trying to pretend is out of the question for me. I've got to do something that I feel deeply. But I think art helps us preserve our balance about our situation. I was at school when I realised that the sun was going to engulf the earth and I thought, well you've got to see everything in that context.

Your poems always seem poised on a cusp, between knowing and not knowing, between the science and the art, between some kind of spiritual certainty and doubt.

Herbert Read says 'you must never be over-sure'. It seems to me that what we really know is usually something very simple, very small: what's important to us now. I'm not aiming at certainty. I would hate to be absolutely sure! That's why I can't adopt a particular religious doctrine, although I'm not anti-religious. I think of religious doctrines as languages – temporary, like all languages, useful but also dangerous. I can't cope with religious confidence about things I think we just can't know. I'm more comfortable being on the edge.

You're suspicious of orthodoxy.

Very. I can't believe something *because* somebody tells me. I can only believe it if I've felt it myself. That's probably why I'm a Quaker. And even then I know one can feel all sorts of things that are not true. But if it's productive in terms of survival I'm willing to give it house-room.

Is reading itself a spiritual experience?

Seldom. Reading Wallace Stevens, I've been aware of feeling that wavering line between one's own reality and the reality outside; of what he calls 'the poem of the mind in the act of finding / What will suffice'. Vaughan in his way does it too. And some of my contemporaries: Tony Connor, Philip Gross, Daphne Gloag, Jeremy Hooker, Ruth Bidgood, Fiona Owen... But it doesn't often happen for me in reading, actually; it happens when I'm out there responding to something myself. And you can't make it happen; it just does.

Can you say whether you privilege one sense over another? Both your parents were artists...

I've often wondered about this. I think sight is crucial. But music is very important to me. And listening to music I have had experiences of a mystical nature. For me it's usually happened through looking carefully and responding to what's outside me:

you suddenly find that you've crossed the border between yourself and it. Only when you come back into yourself do you realize that you've had an experience... I want to say 'of the oneness' [*laughs*]; because that's what it feels like. You can't say it, but you never forget and it lies under or beyond what you can say.

The attempt to transfer what you're describing into words, onto paper, seems doomed to me: how do you pin down the inexpressible in language?

By making holes with words for what aren't words. Trying to make space for, admit, as much of such experience as possible. It's very hard to express this idea, even. It would be wouldn't it? Studying linguistics makes you realise that there's never a one-to-one relationship between a word and its referent. As my friend and mentor the academic William Haas used to say, words are things you walk with, like your legs. They're tools. You use your language to get somewhere.

Which makes it sound organic.

Well we're born into language. Writing should reach out. I've always felt I haven't earned my living if I haven't written – made – something: as if I haven't done my job. Yet I have these doubts about what language can do.

Is that productive?

It feeds into my pleasure in the marginal. I mean, if I wrote in French (which is my first language) I'd be writing something different because of the nature of the language. As the linguist Edward Sapir says, languages have their own structure. You can only do certain things but you want to be on the edge of what language can do the whole time. Not necessarily by being obscure! I like to get the details clear, and leave what things mean and how they connect open to the reader. I think of the poem as a means of exploration for me and for anyone else – getting somewhere you weren't before.

When did you start writing?
I was certainly writing long things by the time I was seven, and always poems, in English. I've never written poetry in French.

You were born on the Continent; the poems in Water to Breathe *have you arriving in this country by boat...*
Yes. Dover, before I was three; we went to Somerset. It was funny really: my father had been ill so he'd grown a beard. He wasn't allowed to shave it off because that was the image on his passport, so people would see this chap with a red beard, think him a spy and report him to the police. Because he was an 'alien' we weren't supposed to move. In the end one night we flitted to Kirkcudbright, where artists like Robert Colquhoun were living. I think we were there for four years or so; then we went to Henley-on-Thames. But by the time I was fourteen we were in Ireland. Just a few of many moves.

You've still got an accent.
My mother was Scottish. She spoke French fluently but her accent was pretty awful; it was easier to talk in English to her. My dad spoke English fluently but with a strong French accent. I spoke French with a French-speaking Swiss nurse. And I was teased for my accent at boarding school, so I deliberately emphasised it.

If I'd asked you at fourteen what you wanted to be, what would you have said?
Poet. By the time I was seven I knew that.

So school interfered?
Well yes. I read a lot of poetry that my mother gave me, anthologies and things. She knew many poems by heart and she used to read to me too: she read the whole of *The Old Curiosity Shop* to me and things like that, and I was writing a lot of poems. She read what I was writing. She was very important to me, because she took it all very seriously.

What sort of a person was she?

She was very self-contained. She'd had a Victorian upbringing and she thought men came first. I remember telling her that I could never agree with a man just because he said something; I'd have to *really agree* with him. And she said, "You'd better be careful about getting married then". It wasn't the sort of thing she'd come out with normally but it was heartfelt. She was a product of her time, but she thought a lot, read a lot. She was a wonderful mother; she really helped me develop. Without her I don't know if I'd have done anything. But I did see that she had been stopped from continuing to develop as an artist. She'd been a professional painter and designer of stained-glass windows, and had a studio in London before she met my father but she never painted while I knew her. That affected my view of marriage. He was a more exploratory painter than she was, but she was very good in her way and it must have meant a lot to her over many years.

Did she betray any frustration?

She just said, 'two temperaments in one house don't go'. And she put him first. She didn't seem to be resentful, but I resented it on her behalf. I thought, I'm not having it done to me.

What about your father?

His importance for me was the way he worked. He always said, Michelangelo couldn't say, 'I don't feel like it today'. I think one ought to sit down at a certain time and try to write. Nothing may come but you have to try. I couldn't disturb him when he was working. He painted every morning for at least three hours, but he spent the rest of the day thinking, often reworking. He showed me you could devote your life to doing something well.

Why Ireland, then?

He wanted to go back to Belgium after the war but there were restrictions in England on taking his pictures with him. If you were living in Ireland, you could take everything back with you. So we bought a house on a river in the West of Ireland, in a place

called Oughterard, and he built a huge studio there. I was at
school in Athlone.

Did you learn Irish?
Yes. I enjoyed Irish very much: I was never fluent in it but I could
write essays. I had to get a decent mark in Irish to be able to go
to university. They wanted to go back to Belgium and, coming up
for 17, I didn't want to. I couldn't go to university in Belgium
without Greek, which I didn't know. For all my interest in them,
in words, I don't learn languages easily. I said I'd stay in Ireland.

Who with?
On my own. In Dublin. They went off and I started a four-year
honours degree at Trinity in French and English literature. I was
sorry to see my mother go, but I had begun to find family life a
bit oppressive. And I saw them in the holidays, at least once a
year.

Did you read Irish poetry?
I learned Irish poetry; I didn't write poems in Irish. But I thought
that you *learned* to write at university – I assumed it was like art
school, so I was astonished that people were there just to read
other people's stuff. Then I found a poetry group and joined that.
The poet Donald Davie supported it. He was a lecturer there
then. I didn't like his poetry much, but he was an excellent
teacher, and very supportive to us as young poets: he took us
seriously, would read and discuss our work with us.

And in 1961 you became an Irish citizen. Why?
Because I felt more at home in Ireland than anywhere else. Of
course I knew I wasn't at home, but I wasn't really Belgian either,
and I wasn't English; somehow I was more European than
English. But I thought Ireland was wonderful. I loved Irish poetry
and I found the literary folk in Dublin very open to a young poet
trying to write. People like Monk Gibbon, Austin Clarke.

Did you know Patrick Kavanagh?

Yes I did.

How did you get to know him?
From sitting in pubs! There was a lot of boozing. I admired
Kavanagh. He was a difficult character but he'd read your stuff.
I remember having some poems published in the Saturday *Irish
Times*, and he recognised me in the pub, and came over and
made some remark about a poem. He let me know that it was
worth looking at but if there was something he didn't like in a
poem he would comment, often humorously. I remember once
I'd written about Dublin Bay's 'almond breakers blossoming' – a
line I was especially proud of! Paddy came over, leant towards me
as he left the pub and said 'I liked your nut crackers'! Maybe
that's why I wanted to be Irish, because other people were
discussing poetry all the time. If you said you were a poet they
didn't say 'O, how interesting'. The nearest I've got to that atmosphere since then has been here, in Abergavenny.

What other poets were about then?
At first there was a group who were older, ex-RAF, and were
about to leave. Many were writing poetry: Michael Srigley, who
went on to lecture in Uppsala. Michael's magazine *Icarus* led me
to get involved, later, in magazines like *Sheaf* and *Scintilla*. I met
Richard Weber, and got to know Tom Kinsella; I admired their
work. When I was about to be dropped from a Swallow anthology of new Irish poets, edited by Donald Carroll, I was grateful
to hear that Tom Kinsella had defended my inclusion. I think he
said something like 'if she's not Irish what is she?'

What about Heaney; was he around then?
Not at that time. But Derek Mahon was a student at Trinity when
I went back to lecture there.

And whose work did you discuss?
We certainly talked about Dylan Thomas – I got to know Michael
Srigley when we heard of Thomas' death at the same moment
and found we both knew his work well. Yeats, Kavanagh, Austin

Clarke. I was also fascinated by people like Goethe and
Yevtushenko, Akhmatova, Mayakovsky, in translation. At that
time the Movement was dominant in England, and it didn't give
me very much – I think I did learn precision, but I couldn't agree
with Davie that one should write poems one would not be
embarrassed to read to a stranger on a train! I loved Marianne
Moore and Elizabeth Bishop, for example. Wallace Stevens of
course. And Stevie Smith.

Do you still feel Irish, today?
I still feel connected, I think because of those first four years on
my own at the university when my parents had gone back to
Belgium. That's when you grow up; when you become yourself.
I still have many friends over there.

I think your first book had an Irish publisher, Dolmen Press?
Yes, Liam Miller's fine press. I was in the Swallow anthology, and
much later in Salmon's *An Phileog Bhan/The White Page*, an
anthology of women poets edited by Joan McBreen. It was Joan
who said I was one of the first women to be considered seriously
in Ireland as a publishing poet. But I'm amphibious, aren't I? I'm
very chuffed to be in Meic Stephens' 1900-2000 Library of
Wales anthology.

Amphibious is a good word for it...
Well I've never liked the word 'alien'. I've always thought it a
rather antagonistic word. I don't mind 'stranger' so much.

But you're not strange here?
Well it's rather like Dublin; I've got a group of poets who are
close like Graham Hartill, Hilary Llewellyn-Williams, Fiona
Owen, Jerry Hooker, Ric Hool... But it's taken time to establish.
And it's not all been easy. I was once asked to submit poems to
an anthology of poets in Wales, and was assured – when I
checked – that I was eligible, although I wasn't Welsh, only to be
rejected for writing about nature rather than industry and 'not
being Welsh enough'. That felt racist. It upset me very much.

You came to Wales just over twenty years ago. Why here?
I was teaching at Sheffield Polytechnic and we had a smallhold-
ing in Penistone, between Barnsley, Huddersfield and Sheffield.
We're not farmers; it was just the house and some fields, but we
like having animals about the place. I didn't like what was
happening at Sheffield (it was a time of cut-backs) and was
wanting to focus on poetry. We saw this place in 1987. We'd been
to the Forest of Dean and loved the country around here; particularly the bare mountains, the Beacons, and the variety along the
rivers and the coast. And I liked the idea of a Celtic country. As
we were both retiring, it was important that we could make a
business here: so we started off doing bed-and-breakfast, and
then moved into the self-catering side of things.

And that seemed to work for the writing.
I really hit my stride when I came to Wales. But it didn't happen
at once. I remember it well: I was forcing myself to write a poem
and getting absolutely nowhere. I thought, that's it then; I'll just
enjoy myself, not write. Whatever there was, it's gone. And I went
to get a coffee, and halfway down the corridor these lines starting coming and I dashed back and wrote them down. That was
the beginning of the 'Timeslips' sequence and the interest in
geology, which I returned to in *Migrations*. But those first poems
arose out of the feeling of being on a border; on the edge,
amongst changes. I liked that. I didn't feel uncomfortable.

In a sense you haven't really stopped writing about Wales, ever since...
Well I've been here longer than anywhere else. I guess that I think
of Wales as on a border between land and sea, not having its feet
flat on the ground all the time. The way I experienced English
culture (middle-class, I suppose), people seemed to know exactly
what was what, how everything should be. I hate that. I didn't
know Wales before we moved, other than being attracted, largely
through reviewing for *Stand*, to poems from Wales. But I felt
comfortable here. Because when I'm in England people think I'm
English, unless they have a good ear and can hear the French in
my accent. And when I'm here people think I'm English and

therefore I'm not Welsh. That feels honest to me, because I'm not
English and nor am I Welsh. Nor Belgian.

So being different feels safer for you?
I feel more comfortable openly standing on that ground.
Being other.
Being not *of*. Just being. I could so easily have been brought up a
bourgeois Belgian. Would I have been the same person? It's
almost impossible to think so. It's the context: natural selection!
What would have been selected in me by a Belgian environment
and my upper-class arty family (although they weren't of the
culture either: the Cluysenaars came from Flirsch in the Austrian
Tyrol). I'm comfortable with people treating me as a stranger: I
am a stranger, after all.

Is this area Wales for you? Or do you go farther afield?
I think of Wales being on an edge, and myself as being on the
edge of Wales. I love to go along the Pembrokeshire coastal path
and inland to the Brecon Beacons. I don't know how it would feel
to live in a Welsh-speaking area. I've tried to learn Welsh. I love
the sounds and being partly French I don't find them hard to
make. As in Irish there are consonants and gutturals you don't
get in English: I like them. I love anything that's different from
the language I speak myself.

*Is it partly that your Wales can be whatever you can make it, do you
think?*
I'd rather think about what *nature* here, or anywhere else, can give
me. I love the Welsh mountains. Thinking about Gwyn Williams
again, and why I like what I imagine of Wales, what comes to
mind is the contrast between straight Roman roads as against the
inter-twinings of Celtic paths (not over-riding the natural
landscape) and Celtic design – the art of the Book of Kells; and
here in Wales movable trefs as against immobile cities: the sense
of another world within this one, into which one may slip or of
which one may not even be aware. I think of reason as needing to
make spaces for the perception of realities which reason itself

may not be able to discover. Exploration beyond whatever may at any point be discoverable. Perhaps this bears on my liking for sequences, the way they offer 'gaps', and – more recently – improvisation, while I've been writing my two-year poem diary.

And this is all to do with a specifically Welsh 'nature' or landscape?
Take Wales' unique geology. All the great geologists, British or other, developed their ideas in Wales: Murchison and Lyell and so on. Because of the mountains and the way the land has folded; the valleys even changed direction! It's a quite astonishing part of the planet from that point of view, once you start realising how rocks move and change, and how they liquefy under certain kinds of pressure. When one folds on top of another the younger rocks end up below the older ones. Rock is a glimpse of what actually happened at some time. We'll leave traces behind; we just don't know what will survive. It's wonderful when you turn up a fossil and see bodily details, like the eyes of a trilobite. Anything that no longer exists, but was probably living before human beings began and may have been part of what led to us.

You could photograph it, say; but you choose to write a poem about it.
Yes. Because it's not only what you see visually; it's what you feel about what you see and the way language works with time, with sequence. A good photograph of a trilobite is a lovely thing but I wouldn't feel as strongly about it as I would if I'd found a fossil in a stone. It's the reality that's outside you, all the time, that fascinates me.

Is Wales something you are outside, then, turning over like that?
Big geological changes don't respect boundaries, they don't respect the existence of a place called Wales or Ireland. It makes you realize that there are more essential things than the boundaries we put up.

And you've crossed some of those boundaries. Out of choice.
Not only choice. But look, we can use language to think about this. You can say in French that somebody's *trés sympathetique*.

You can't say that in English. I'm interested in how structures resist or encourage experience, even though you need those same structures to explore experience.

You say you're not political, but this is sounding political...
What worries me about political systems and dogmas is that we fight each other over them. I wish we didn't have to. I remember hearing at a reading in the Valleys a poem about seducing an English girl because, being English and middle-class, she deserved it. I was shocked: that's the sort of thing I really hate. But many Welsh nationalists are open to other ways of seeing the world; they don't dismiss you because you come from somewhere else. I voted for independence because I felt that that kind of racist nationalism might be overcome by Wales having more of its own say. Belgium incorporates Flemish and French, and all the tensions between the two cultures, languages and religions.

And being in that in-between space is productive?
I feel protected here, by how people respond to me. Meic Stephens' willingness to put me in an anthology mattered to me, and not only personally. It suggests a wider notion of what poets from Wales may be, as opposed to 'Welsh poets'. I can't stand anywhere and say "I belong here, and you lot don't". There are a lot of people like me. It doesn't mean that we don't belong in the world; we just don't have a particular badge to wear.

I hear this very strongly in your collection Migrations. *Are you conscious of seeking out this subject – cultural difference, or strangeness, boundaries, whatever – as a theme?*
I don't plan poems. I get a kind of feeling, almost like a tune, which I can't describe; I just know that there's a poem there. I can't think, I ought to write about this theme. But when linguists – some of them – say that we can only 'see' the world through language, that seems to me rubbish. I feel as though there's something more inevitable about Nature than the things we set up, like houses, like languages, like behaviours. It's not language

that makes the world real, though it does affect what we pay attention to and feel easiest in saying: the thing exists and you hope you get some of its resistance into the poem. Wittgenstein says that 'whereof we cannot speak, thereof we must be silent'. The opposite is true for poets. What you can't speak of won't stay silent: you must try to make language at least gesture towards it.

Thank you, Anne.

1. A shortened version of this interview, which has since been revised, appeared in *Poetry Wales* No. 44. issue 3 pp. 27-30.
2. Dr George Beccaloni was curator of orthopoteroid insects in the Department of Entomology at the Natural History Museum of London.

MENNA ELFYN

Menna Elfyn has produced nine volumes of poetry with her Welsh-language publishers Gwasg Gomer: *Mwyara* (1976); *'Stafelloed Aros* (1978); *Tro'r Haul Arno* (1982); *Mynd Lawr i'r Nefoedd* (1986); *Aderyn Bach Mewn Llaw* (1990); *Eucalyptus* (1995); *Perffaith Nam* (2005); *Er Dy Fod* (2007); and the retrospective selection *Merch Perygl: Cerddi 1976-2011* (2011). Her bilingual (translated) collections include *Eucalyptus: Detholiad o Gerddi / Selected Poems 1978–1994* (Gomer, 1995); *Cusan Dyn Dall / Blind Man's Kiss* (Bloodaxe, 2001); *Perfect Blemish: New & Selected Poems / Perffaith Nam: Dau Ddetholiad & Cherddi Newydd 1995-2007* (Bloodaxe, 2007); and *Murmur* (Bloodaxe, 2012). She co-edited *The Bloodaxe Book of Modern Welsh Poetry* (2003, with John Rowlands), and has also published plays, libretti and children's novels. She lives in Llandysul, Ceredigion and is Professor of Poetry at Trinity St Davids in Lampeter.

As someone who can only read you in English, I wanted to start with the language issue. Does speaking Welsh make it simpler for you, for anyone, to be "Welsh"?
Well this might surprise you, but although I write in Welsh and speak Welsh, and speak Welsh at home, and my kids are Welsh-speaking and I live in what is apparently the Welshest part of Welsh-speaking Wales, I still have a problem with identity, in the same way perhaps as people who don't speak Welsh.

How can that be?
Because although I speak and write in Welsh, I sense myself an

outsider even within my Welsh language community. I was brought up in the Swansea valley and went to a school where there was no Welsh at all; I'd speak English in school, and Welsh at home and in Chapel. At that time – the fifties – Welsh was deemed a dying language; even when we moved near Carmarthen we had merely one lesson a day in Welsh at school. But I'd go home and I'd only hear Welsh, and I spoke Welsh with my friends there. But we tended to speak English with each other in the schoolyard. And then again, although I was proud of being Welsh, I wanted to prove that I could speak English as well as the next person. I think that's why I talk quickly in English now: I always thought that to speak slowly in English made you sound like a Welsh person from the back of beyond. And finally the Welsh I spoke to my peers was different from theirs, because I was brought up in the Manse, where we were taught by my dad that there was a Welsh word for every English word. So I didn't use anglicised words in my Welsh; I spoke a kind of pure Welsh, which marked me out.

You don't have to apologise any longer though, do you?
Well I feel that Welshness as a label, an identity, is far more pronounced now: people are more proud of it, there's not the stigma and the feeling of second class citizenship that I grew up with and that we battled as a Welsh language society. But on the other hand, the Welsh language is diminishing in its quality, in the sense of what I can achieve in writing poetry in Welsh. Enriching the language is becoming more problematic as it declines in another sense. Being translated has given me a new freedom to push the limits of the language; to write the way I want to write, regardless of my audience. You'll know that there are different kinds of poetry in Wales. There's the strict poetry of *cynghanedd*, which poets love to write for contests and is very rich, but it can sometimes seem claustrophobic. I remember it being introduced to me, at university, as a rather esoteric kind of poetry. If you didn't understand it, that didn't matter; it felt as if there wasn't any need to understand because it wasn't for you to understand. Although of course I'm being simplistic about this; many people

admire this way of writing, for its sound and intricacy, but I wanted to connect with the world. To be free to write as I wanted. When I started writing, I didn't have the time or the patience to learn the craft of *cynghanedd*. It depends on learning the rules, and on having a mentor, a '*meuryn*' or teacher. And the way I wanted to write, at the time of women's so-called liberation, was also totally at odds with the bardic male tradition. Nowadays of course women take part in this, but not then. So I was always an outsider in poetry; for me writing was an outsider's world and Welsh was the only language at my disposal. It still is.

You were quite activist weren't you? I associate activism with passion, even anger. Do you still feel angry about living in a cultural environment which can still feel embattled?
Yes but I think that being an activist dissolved that anger, so it became conciliatory; in fact I prefer to call it 'passion' or 'constructive impatience' at the system. I wrote a poem about going to prison for the language but coming to new causes there because you meet women there who have no language at all; who can't articulate anything. I think the more activist you are the more you come to new understandings. Breaking the law at that time made us feel we were part of the movement of changing the world! It might sound crazy now but in the sixties we really did think we were changing the power structures: we were part of a movement trying to renegotiate the world through street politics, from anti-apartheid to cutting a fence in Brawdy or going to Greenham Common. Being a pacifist also meant that non-violent protest was just as important as the causes we believed in.

Can we talk about Wales, rather than Welshness? What is Wales for you? Somewhere – anywhere – where Welshness can be found? Or is it perhaps imaginary?
It's imaginary. It's a desire.

Does it have borders?
The strange thing is, I like to be both outside and within; I suppose that's the dilemma of the writer. Sometimes I feel that I

write about what I hope to believe in even if I can't live in it yet.
I think my poetry is where my humanity is, and it's where I think.
That's why desire is a good word for what one hopes to achieve
in poetry; the desire to have a world you can live within. I think
it also explains those great poets who perhaps weren't exemplary
human beings: poetry allows you to reach another realm that
redeems all your failings. It's the 'other person' you hope to find.
And at times you're surprised to see it there, completed, on the
page: an entirely different kind of 'you'.

But Wales is your home.
Yes. But I'm sometimes restless when at home and when I'm
away, I'm full of *hiraeth* or longing. The original meaning of
'hiraeth' is a long piece of land – I suppose that's also my idea of
Wales.

So it's imagined but it's also present.
Yes: it is the only place where I want to live. But I also like being
out of Wales. I hate the idea of the cosiness, the close-knit
community, although I'm proud when I see it in action. I don't
think writers are very good at dealing with being hemmed-in in
a certain community, whether it's a language community or a
country, which is why I often say that Wales, being such a small
country, is just one large parish really. Whenever I'm in North
Wales I feel at home; in fact regardless of what R.S. Thomas says,
in one of his poems, there's nowhere I won't go.

You have travelled a lot. Does being away make you like it more?
[*Laughing.*] Yes I like Wales much more when I'm away from it. I
think I'm afraid of being confined to a place. And when I travel
it's also the time when I'm, spiritually, elsewhere. That sense of
being elsewhere is sometimes better than being somewhere. It's
where I can find a temple within me which is where I also belong;
when I know I'm from Wales, even when I'm in other places. In
a way, Wales is the elsewhere that is waiting for me, that I long for.

Linguistically you're much less well-travelled in a way; although

many of your poems have been translated into English, you've written
very little in English yourself. I'm guessing that's deliberate? Or is it
that you actually can't write – or not as you'd want – in English?
The very few poems I've written in English have always been out
of necessity – there's been a sudden commission, which leaves no
time for handing it over to a translator and waiting for their
version. So I admit I've dabbled; but it's only dabbling, not the
real thing. I recently wrote a poem to be placed on trams in Hong
Kong called 'Lightness'. It had to be done quickly. I then translated it into Welsh and it sounded better, because it was then my
voice; I wasn't using a borrowed tongue. I fear falling more and
more into English with all the travelling. The terror attached to
that is of losing the language – Welsh – that gives me inspiration
and sustenance. So I suppose that's why I like living where I live,
because that's where I hear the language. I'm the kind of writer
who if she doesn't hear the language feels like she's in exile. When
I spent some time working in New York City I found myself
talking to the walls in my hotel room because there was no one I
could speak to and I wanted, needed, a conversation even if it was
between four walls. So language is also an environment and not
an instrument, to quote Philippe Vasset; I need Wales for my
language to live within it.

Do words like 'transnational' or 'transcultural' threaten that kind of
linguistic identification, for you?
I know that the more I travel the more I realise how many people,
like me, have this double-bind, treble-bind, working within the
language and struggling with it at the same time. With globalisa-
tion most people compare their lives with other cultures. When
he was at college, my son overheard another student say 'This
guy is Welsh. Really really Welsh. He's so Welsh he could almost
be Romanian'! That to me captures the essence of our lives: we
can only compare one culture in recognising another. Talk about
the 'Other'; it's all there, in that one quip.

How important is the struggle to you as a writer, to your writing?
I think struggle is part of the writer's world. Not 'angst' struggle

but a sense of tension; of wondering, can I persist or exist as a Welsh-language poet for my entire life? The sales of my work in Spanish far exceed my Welsh-language sales. That worries me: that the language I'm writing in is less 'received' by the language community I'm writing for, in a way. Although if I write for them, I also write for myself and others; for, as Mary Oliver says, 'strangers hundreds of years away who might stumble on a poem'. I don't underestimate the challenges of Welsh surviving as a vibrant literary language, but I also want *more of* the language. I want myself – my poems – to *do* more with the language rather than accept it as a medium. I want it to be on the world literature stage. *Cell Angel* has been translated into Norwegian and *Perfect Blemish* into Hindi, as well as a new chapbook in Chinese called 'Door in Epynt', that was mistranslated as 'Door in Egypt'! So, little things get lost or reimagined too in another language which is sometimes comical and sometimes makes sense to that language community. But I'm just as proud of my *Selected* in Welsh, *Merch Perygl* [*Danger's Daughter* or *Danger's Woman*], and of *Murmur*, which was a Poetry Book Society Recommended Translation. It's the first-ever book of Welsh language poetry in English translation to be selected. It was lovely for me and my translators to be recognised in that way.

Thinking about that world stage, what about the so-called 'British Isles'? Does Wales' relationship with her neighbours trouble or interest you?
I think we have a new kind of understanding. Back in the eighties when I started to be invited to festivals in Edinburgh and Galway and so on, I sensed an affinity with Gaelic and Irish. One model when I started translating was Nuala ní Dhomhnail: she did the translation in parallel texts before me, although that was far more necessary in Irish than in Welsh. You could still have a viable literary life in Wales writing Welsh only. But there was great deal of resistance when I started publishing parallel texts. [*Laughs.*] Oh God...

How much of that resistance was gendered do you think?

Some (women) critics maintain that a lot of it was gendered. But
the late R. Gerallt Jones, a wonderful writer, argued that the
Welsh-language community's resistance to translation was due
partly to self-protection ('this is ours and nobody writes like this
anywhere else in the world') and partly to a fear that Welsh
perhaps wouldn't clean up as well in English. And that sense of
fear I think was part of it. I was opening a gate or a door they
didn't want opened. Now everybody's translating or writing
books in Welsh and English, and nobody says anything, but at the
time what I was trying to do was seen as a kind of betrayal. The
more I've travelled the more I've realised that it goes with the
territory; I've seen it in other countries. People want to own you
and want to keep you in your place at the same time. Perhaps
being a woman made it easier for me to move out of a place I
never belonged in anyway. I refused to be translated until 1989
because I didn't think I *myself* was ready for that 'opening up'.
And, knowing that, I didn't feel ready to make a shift leading to
what some exiled writers have called 'a second life'.

I'm glad of the translations and enjoy them, but I'd much rather be
able to read the originals. Do you want me to think of the translations
as being as valid as your poems?
Yes. I love my translations and they're done by acclaimed poets
who really care for the language and poetry. You can't ask for
more. I allow them freedom to invent; sometimes they can see
something that perhaps I didn't. Or didn't want them to see! I
just love the act of translation. I'm translating Gillian Clarke's
National Poet poems myself. The Afrikaans writer Antjie Krog
has described how important language proved in South Africa,
during apartheid, when as she says 'people (were) desperate to
find one another after so many years of being kept apart. To stay
in your language meant to stay a part.'[1] That was my feeling,
when I began; the need for translation caught me unaware,
because people wanted to read my work. In *The Bloodstream*
(1989) I'm called an 'established Welsh poet'. I didn't feel that at
the time, but I wanted to connect with the English-speaking
majority, who through no fault of their own didn't speak Welsh.

Translation became a way to connect with that majority. Antjie says 'I wanted to be and become part of the new South Africanness which was being formed.'[2] In a way, that was my own sentiment: because of the miners' strike, and CND, peace campaigns and so on, I was involved more and more with people who didn't speak Welsh but were part of those other aspirations.

Translation takes us – you – to another place, doesn't it, and I'm not thinking here about another linguistic culture necessarily; I mean it seems as if it takes you, as a writer, into a different creative domain...
Being translated allows you what Yeats called the 'fascination with what's difficult'; you can't get more 'difficult' than trying to reach from one language to another. I love Mourid Barghouti's idea that translation cools language down. It's also such a wonderful way of learning the craft of writing. I think we're all born to translate whether we do it well or not. I can't read Rilke or Lorca without having one ear in tune with how it would resonate in Welsh. Strange as that may seem.

It attracts you, that sense of estrangement; it doesn't seem or feel disempowering?
Not it's not disempowering. In fact it's quite appealing as you say.

You're looking mischievous.
[*Laughs.*] It's that sense of still being radical and still pushing boundaries and still being restless. I think restlessness is part of the process of translation. When you have debates and so on, it's another way of thinking and it makes you more agile and more aware of what you've just written.

So it's both collaborative and empowering.
Yes, well, it enriches. No: it's another instrument of enrichment.

Maybe that's because you are bilingual? Because I can't read you in Welsh, I can't hear you; I can't sound you out.
Well I think a lot of poets depend on sound. I love sound. I want to make music in poetry and that's what I want from my transla-

tors. If they can get the music across then I think, we're almost there. Welsh and Irish poetry, and other poetries of course, because of their histories, depended on music and accompaniment and I love the idea of work that sings. I may have written more libretti in the last ten years than poetry. Keeping in tune with music and working with composers is another form of translation. An even more complex one at times.

I was interested to find R.S. Thomas translating you, but his version of your poem 'Message' (Eucalyptus) seemed very dark. How did that collaboration come about?

We used to write to each other. (I've kept half a dozen of his letters; I never thought to keep others. But you don't think, in your twenties and thirties, that something you write or receive is going to be important.) But he only translated two of my poems. I asked him when I was fined fifty pounds for some campaign or other. I wanted to send a translation to the authorities instead of the fine. His letter back said, 'You know what I feel about translation. It shouldn't be done. If people can't read it in the original then forget it.' And then, at the very bottom, '...but I've done my best', and overleaf was 'Song of a Voiceless to British Telecom' (*Eucalyptus*), in English. Later on I wrote and said 'I've got one of your poems in a forthcoming book (my first book); it looks a bit odd that there's only one. Would you do me another?' And he said yes, but 'I don't want to choose; you send one that you want me to do.' I thought of 'Message'. My Welsh has it as 'there was something in us as a people that was wanting to die'; his 'death-wish' is something else really. But I didn't mind, because he was R.S.!

So, it was quite a political meeting-up then: it wasn't a natural collaboration.

No... Tony Conran was different. I kept all his letters because I needed to: they were intellectual, probing, full of queries and suggestions. He'd write reams. One time he wrote it as an exam paper: 'what does the poet mean by' [chuckles]. It was inspirational: his enthusiasm gave me renewed confidence that I really was on the right track and he often sensed or saw things I didn't. I'm not sure any of us fully appreciated his achievements as a translator or poet. It was his *Penguin Book of Welsh Poetry* (1967) which inspired me back in the sixties to try and write in the first place. He gave so much to Welsh literature, in a time when Wales was little understood by people who couldn't read its poetry.

I suppose, having come from a very lonely place, that I think of my translators as my poetic community: they're the ones I trust. When I translate my own poems into English I find I try to make a new poem, and forget what I was after in the Welsh, so it moves away from translation. I have an understanding with my translators, and I think they always know what's acceptable with me and what's not.

I think it makes you seem very generous-spirited, but not everyone approves, do they? Do you mind that?
I think every poet who tries to do something different will get knocks. You just have to be true to what you think really. I love Leonard Cohen's belief that if you do something for long enough, in the end, people will come round to it. Of course, I'm lucky: I have a good following and my Welsh readership serves me well. Adrienne Rich says that writing comes out of a sense of necessity; that's really my feeling...

You've said that Blind Man's Kiss *was one of your best collections. Do you still think this and, if so, why?*
Well I think of that volume as being edgy, and not conforming. And I think that comes from my non-conformist background. My dad was a Minister, a radical preacher and a socialist, and I have called myself a Christian anarchist before now. That comment still haunts me wherever I go in the world, but the sense of being anarchic still appeals. That's why I write poetry I suppose: it's going against the grain, against the rush of time. Anyway I now think that *Murmur* is my best book and strangely it's far more Welsh-centred than *Blind Man's Kiss*. Which shows you just how inconsistent writers can be!

*What about more recent work; are you conscious of your work chang-
ing as you get older? Even if the principles – the vision, perhaps –
don't change, does the work itself? Or does it change you?*
There is always the tendency of writing the same kind of poem,
without being aware of it. That's why I relish new challenges like
libretti or drama: they stop me getting too obsessed with writing
poetry. It probably takes a few years to gather enough for a book
of poetry; I'm hoping my next one will be far more innovative in
style.

*Would your younger self have been surprised to find herself so
questioning and radical (contentious, even) a writer do you think?*
Well I always wanted to be a writer. And I was a loner; although
I had a few friends, my best friend was me. And poetry. I felt that
from a very early age, but especially from the end of primary
school, moving to another setting, always writing on my own:
trying to articulate and make sense of the world. There's a poem
in *Blindman's Kiss* about not being able to say my 'r's; being
Welsh-speaking, that was a kind of disgrace. So I used to hate the
fact that, living in a Welsh culture, I couldn't speak the words I
wanted to in an eloquent way. I suppose I battled against that and
in writing eventually broke free. But I was also a very shy person.
I suppose I still am but there is that sense of the necessity of
delivering your poems in such a way that they are allowed to
scatter or fly to listeners in their own way. But I find reading in
public takes a good deal of energy; the desire is often simply to
be still and embrace silence.

Were your parents enabling?
As a teenager I rebelled a lot against my dad, who was authori-
tarian but mellowed as he grew older (and perhaps I mellowed
too of course); we shared the same interest in writing. He's dead
now but I'm still writing poems about him. He was a well-known
hymnist. In fact Bryn Terfel sings one of his great hymns. But my
dad was a very modest man. I remember when I brought him my
first book he said 'Don't forget your modesty.' That was typical
of him. Not, 'This is a good book. Well done.' But he was very

supportive when I ended up in prison. I think he had difficulty with me growing up, with feminism and all of that. But then when people started to question things about my poetry, he quickly became a feminist!

What about your mother?
My mother was very gentle. Very unassuming. As a minister's wife she had to do lots of public things but hated it. She was also very musical. My daughter inherited that. I play the harp and piano and guitar and I used to be in a band but I'm not musically accomplished in the way my daughter Fflur is. My mother could and did play anything. She was a very dedicated mother. Knowing how little Welsh I had in the primary school, she would sit down in the evenings and teach me new words or compound nouns or give me grammatical exercises to do. I owe so much to my mother for her refusal to accept the birthmark – a purple-coloured growth – which grew on my cheek. She went to every hospital in Wales when I was a baby to find someone who would take it seriously. I was lucky that Emlyn Lewis - a pioneer in plastic surgery at Chepstow Hospital – took me on. I was admitted at 18 months old and spent long periods in hospital over the next three years having major face lifts to remake my face. It was a huge success and I traipsed to conferences for years afterwards so he could show me off to other surgeons. So my mother was remarkable: she was shy but very tenacious; she just didn't take no for an answer.

The Wales that your daughter, Fflur [Dafydd], is writing in and about, must seem very different to the one in which you 'battled' for your voice.
Seeing my daughter flourish as a bilingual writer has been really wonderful. I love that she's won more awards than me! We are very close: I read her work and she sometimes reads mine. I proofread her Welsh and she proofreads my English. I'll send her a bunch of poems to ask her opinion and likewise she'll send me drafts of her work for me to comment on. That complete honesty is invaluable. We teach creative writing at universities not far

away from one another (Swansea and Trinity St David's) so we talk shop as well. That her English is so superb gives me a great feeling. Ironically she went to a mostly Welsh-medium school and writes in English, whereas I went to an English-medium school and can only write poetry in Welsh...

Do you think you face different issues or bring different perspectives to bear on them?
Our subject matter is completely different. But her last few books have been European in texture, and I suppose my poetry too in some sense is European. But I'm influenced by American poetry and deeply interested in theology and philosophy. Although we're close, there is a sense of distance between us as writers. The understanding between us keeps us close but also keeps us guessing.

Can you tell me a bit about the kinds of projects you're planning, or are coming up? What's exciting you at the moment?
I thoroughly enjoyed writing the libretto for 'Gair ar Gnawd', an oratorio by the wonderful composer Pwyll ap Siôn; Welsh National Opera Max are going to be touring with it in 2015, so I'm looking forward to that. I have a play in the making but it will be some time before that's finished. My new book will be in Welsh but it's hard to talk about it right now. But above all I was aware that I travelled so much during 2013; I wanted to avoid that if I could. So it feels good to have the possibility to 'be still' for a while; though I'm not sure – perhaps that too will turn out to be a desire...

Thank you very much, Menna.

1. Antjie Krog, *The Poetry Papers* (2008/09):22

CHRISTINE EVANS

Christine Evans has authored seven full-length collections of poetry: *Looking Inland* (Seren, 1983); *Falling Back* (Seren, 1986); *Cometary Phases* (Seren, 1989); *Island of Dark Horses* (Seren, 1995); *Selected Poems* (Seren, 2004); *Growth Rings* (Seren, 2006); and *Burning the Candle* (Gomer, 2006). She has written a variety of other books, including a book of short stories for children and the illustrated study *Bardsey* (Gomer, 2008). She spent many years teaching English in Pwllheli Grammar School. She lives near Aberdaron on the tip of the Llŷn Peninsula, but spends up to five months of the year on Bardsey Island (*Enlli*), in the home where her husband's family has farmed for generations.

You have described showing some early work to R.S. Thomas. How did that come about?
I think my husband's father, Will Evans [*Wil Ty Pella*] who suggested I show R.S. some work. It would have been in about 1969. I'd never thought about writing for an audience other than myself; I was writing to make sense of my own life. In about 1975, quite abruptly, out of the euphoria of giving birth and feeling like a proper woman, secure in that role, I began writing about the community I was living in.

How did your father-in-law come to know R.S.?
R.S. used to come over to Bardsey Bird Observatory, and Wil and his son – my husband Ernest – ferried him across. R.S.'s poem 'Island Boatman' is about him.

If 'Bonanza' is anything to go by, R.S. wasn't very encouraging. Did you mind?

I remember burning with shame that my thoughts were so ordinary. That's how his comments made me feel. But after that my response was very much the sort of shrug that's in the poem: well, I've plenty of things to get on with. But it wasn't long before I began again. The experience of 'Bonanza' (*Looking Inland*) was very much that: I stumbled over things to write about. I wrote a whole collection, a poem a day, between Christmas and February 1976, all about local people, probably out of a sense of wanting to answer Thomas' own ill-humoured portrayal of country life.

Did you have a mentor or guide?

I would say everybody I've ever read, really, but since I didn't show my writing to anyone, nobody really helped or supported me before Meic Stephens, then editor of *Poetry Wales*. I've still got the 1969 rejection slip – my first – from him saying he'd like to see some more work. And then Cary Archard said, sometime in the 1970s, that they were getting together some pamphlets and had I anything? That turned into *Looking Inland*, my first collection.

How did you come to settle in Wales?

Through accident and family connections. My father was born and grew up in Pwllheli and when he died I came back to teach in the grammar school. It was somewhere for my mother and my family to start again. With hindsight I see it was naively optimistic idea, to uproot and replant a family, but it worked out for me: I met my husband in 1968, married in 1969, and have been in his *cynefin*, his homeplace, ever since.

You were born in Yorkshire. Can you tell me about your childhood?

My father – an instinctive intellectual who had no academic training – was born when his own father (a solicitor) was well into his fifties. He was a conscientious objector during the war and went to prison. He defended himself – I've still got all the papers. When he lost his job after the war, my parents had to move to a cheaper area where there was more work.

Do you remember the move?
I remember the shock of it very clearly. I don't think my mother ever recovered from the public shame of being evicted. She became a recluse. He was a dreamer, trapped. He would escape from the hurly burly of family life from time to time. I don't think he ever understood us. I loved his gentleness and the way he didn't notice trivial things, but I was quite a withdrawn child and we only had two or three serious discussions. I never had time to get to know him. I went off to university and was teaching in North London when he died. In fact I hardly thought about him until I was writing *Burning the Candle* in 2003.

You've written movingly about your mother, mostly from the perspective of her later years and eventual death. What was she like?
She was from a hard-working, Northern working class background, quick at school and eager to learn but not allowed to continue after the age of fourteen because she was a girl. And the only surviving girl of a family of eight – half of whom had died of TB. Her role was to have been to stay at home and look after her parents. Then in her twenties she joined a Ramblers' club and got interested in Esperanto – which is how she met my father and what must have seemed her big chance. In her own way, she was an idealist too, she wanted to change the world and had a fierce sense of justice. But her personal disappointment made her difficult to live with. The struggle was too much for her. It made her bitter.

What kind of a child were you?
I was solitary, an only child, until I was 6; I was probably rather spoilt. School came as a shock and a horror; it made me recoil into myself. My companions up until then had been pets and my imaginary friend Lalla, my grandparents on my father's side, my mother. Ours was a professional middle class family until my grandfather's death revealed that my father, who had no qualifications and had borrowed money to care for my grandfather, was illegitimate and had no right to the business. Everything was lost. I think my mother had a breakdown and things were never the

same again. Family life became a daily improvisation; there was always anxiety over money, about basics like shoes, fuel, even food. My mother's increasingly eccentric behaviour, my father's sporadic disappearances, left us all floundering. And when I was about 13, I saw that education was my way out; from then on I really worked hard at school. I believed if I had a degree I'd never be in the same position as my father.

Your Welsh grandmother lived with you when you were little. Do you remember her well?
I remember her as an emotional presence, really. Of course childhood memories are often constructed but I have a clear picture of her long slow dying in our sitting room, and the scraps of Welsh I kept and muttered to myself afterwards.

Did you always read?
Oh yes. I first read poetry at primary school, encouraged by my headmaster. It was all learning by rote from things like Palgrave's *Golden Treasury*; Victorian verses like 'For I'm to be Queen of the May' and later on 'The Charge of the Light Brigade'. So I was well-grounded in singsong rhythms. Otherwise I read for my studies: D.H. Lawrence, *Sons and Lovers* in particular, and Wordsworth. I decided to study History at university; I switched to English at the last minute.

What difference did university make to the writing you?
Reading the Romantics (even though I'm not very keen on them now) was influential. I loved Keats' imagery and I read a lot of Blake. Baudelaire. I think the studies influenced my *reading*, but if anything, university stopped me *writing*, because what I wanted to write seemed completely out of synch with the things published in the university and English department magazines.

Your working life – as farmer, teacher – has always seemed present in your writing.
I shouldn't have called myself a farmer, though I always wanted to be one. I married the son of a farmer who preferred the sea.

He was a fisherman, really. We have a little land; we don't keep livestock any more. But I think we should get more physical work into poetry. It seems to have become very cerebral, so I like to write about digging and so on.

Working as an English teacher has affected my writing much more than studying English literature. Literature and landscape brought me through my childhood. I don't like the idea that poetry has to come from 'the hurt', as Yeats said, or words to that effect, but in my case it's probably true. My poem 'Adjusting the Focus' (*Growth Rings*) is about trying to make myself small and quiet and unnoticed: [Reads] 'Through words I found a wormhole / I came through to womanhood / that floodplain with its fruiting trees'. The words that saved me were ones I wrote or read. I come back to Wordsworth's sense of nature, the sense of perspective that you get from looking at tens of millions of grains of sand on a beach, or looking up at the stars. No matter how dreadful things are, it doesn't matter in the scheme of things. I got a sense of ordinariness and beauty from Wordsworth that I found nowhere else until I came to Bardsey. And found a place where everything seemed in balance. And the orderliness I craved; the safety within a family. My mother in law washed on Mondays, baked bread three times a week, had dinner on the table at noon every day. The men moved between the farm and the sea, following the weather and the tide. It was predictable, governed by nature.

Do you remember your very first trip to Bardsey? How did you feel?
It felt like discovery, a green place where I could literally take root and grow. In 'Unseen Island' (*Looking Inland*) I call it "my unblurring."

Did you find it easy to fit into the family, and the community?
I was intoxicated by it all at first. I wanted to learn everything, re-invent myself as a practical person. I still get tremendous satisfaction out of practical tasks well done: a well-risen loaf, a brood of healthy ducklings, tomatoes grown from seed. The hardest thing was learning what was not acceptable – talking

about emotions, having wild ideas; behaving out of the ordinary. I came to think of it as rural convention, the strength of the group over individual expression.

Was your mother-in-law a product of this way of life herself or did she have to learn it?
My mother-in-law was a very strong, very straightforward and generous person and I tried to fit into her place, but I lacked her background – frugal, honest, hardworking, above all, stoical. Keep calm and carry on. No outbursts or imaginative indulgences (a recent piece describes a dream she once confided, about flying away south with the shearwaters, but ends with her 'public' face, denying that she ever wasted energy in dreaming.) With hindsight, this reserve might have been a factor in the sudden bubbling-up of poems in the mid 70s.

Can we talk about your writing? You used to record your poems driving in the car.
The feeling comes first and then I find an image to fit: a few words, a phrase spoken out loud. They shape themselves into lines that I jot down, as and when I can, in a notebook I keep in the car. This started when the only time I had for writing – for my own thoughts – was travelling to and from work, a 35-40 minute journey into school and back, on very quiet roads. I used to look forward to that time, when I could just drive and speak out my lines. Recording these 'oral jotting' helped me feel that they weren't lost, they could be retrieved, to help me recall the emotions and (re)capture some of the initial energy of the experience. These days I use a tiny digital voice recorder. Sometimes I compose the first phrases, sometimes read the first drafts. But I hope that I write for the ear. For the tune of the poem.

How did (do) you get from there to the page?
In those days I'd try to get something on paper by the evening. Last thing at night, when everybody else had gone up to bed, I'd sit in the kitchen and read out the lines, see what sort of pattern

they were making and write a first draft, in soft pencil on a big sheet of A4, so there was lots of space around the phrases and the key words. Sometimes these lines were discarded. Sometimes they became the end or a different poem altogether.

Do you find writing hard?
I love the beginning. Like catching something translucent you can't quite see the shape of, until you've got it on paper, and exploring it, working on it to try to keep it alive, keep its energy going. I've written about tending a poem, almost like looking after a baby, in 'Weaning'. I love the sense of discovery, going back again and again. The hardest part is letting go, deciding it's finished. Thinking: 'that's it'.

Who do you think you write for?
I don't have an ideal reader in mind. I touch on this in *Burning the Candle*. Seamus Heaney said that every writer needs 'a group of talented fond mockers' who will look at his work and comment, and I suppose the more you get published the more you need people you can trust who can criticise you. But I'm not in touch with other writers. I don't send work out. I'd like to, I think, but I've always written in isolation.

Your poems have always seemed very confident, formally.
Well I think formal control is very important, although I like to think I write in a speaking voice. Form is just the box that you put the thought in, where the images can grow. And it can be very beautiful. But when the box gets more important than the contents, things can become too stiff, too elaborate. The game takes over.

Do you favour a particular form?
I'm keen on the three line stanza. Perhaps because it's a bit less closed: something can happen in between, in that space where the fourth line would be. I also like loose forms, probably thanks to Americans like Denise Levertov, Galway Kinnell, William Carlos Williams.

How did you come across writers like that?
Radio 3 used to have a regular programme, *Poetry Now*, where
contemporary writers read their own work. In those days, the
70s, I was completely isolated from writing and didn't have spare
cash for books, and that programme was important nourishment.
I remember being transfixed by Kinnell's voice, his cadences and
rhythmic subtlety. He read about a pair of tramp's shoes, and
watching his children sleeping in the moonlight, and I've sought
out his work ever since. I found Levertov on the airwaves too, but
I read William Carlos Williams from the page. I love poetry
readings – John Burnside, Adam Thorpe, Philip Gross, Michael
Longley – but I still prefer the disembodied voice without
performance, the primacy of the words.

*Eavan Boland has described practising particular forms over and
over again. Did you?*
I have played with different forms: sonnets and couplets and
villanelles. But what I think of as the real exploratory work, takes
its form from the tune of those first phrases. For me the short
lyric is a process of clarification and paring down. While you may
not know exactly how it's going to finish, there's a resolution in
that comparatively short space.

And the sequence?
I don't think I have ever written a sequence. To me the long poem
feels freer: like diving in, deep, and not knowing where you'll end
up, whereas the sequence is swimming round and round
something. I enjoy writing the long poem. I'm excited by the
energy it generates. The short lyric is like uncovering something
precious, something furled, rather than striding out...

Why might you use one over the other?
I suppose, if I know what's going to happen. In *Burning the
Candle* I had nothing in mind other than writing about light and
the seven colours of light of the prism. The other things seemed
to crowd in on me. But I don't know that I'll ever write another
long poem. I don't feel compelled, *impelled*. I'd like to try a

sequence, and also much more concise short lyrics

Which of your own poems, short or long, is your favourite?
'Cometary Phases' (*Cometary Phases*) is perhaps my favourite because of the time in my life when it was written. I wasn't nervous about writing it, as I was with *Burning the Candle*, where I was stretching myself, and afraid of getting things wrong. Working by instinct; that felt daring. 'Cometary Phases' had a very straight structure by contrast: those seven occasions when we failed to see Halley's comet.

Burning the Candle *reveals the slog of writing, but it's open about the joys and excitement as well. I like the way it undoes its own processes. Did it surprise you?*
It surprised me every day, constantly suggesting its own unravelling of concerns, offering images and scenes from memory that I simply sorted sections. I was never stuck for material; in fact I was woken in the small hours by urgent lines. A lot of it was scribbled at night, which adds to the sense of the poem as exploration, a groping towards understanding the writing process and beyond that, what it is to be human. Nothing was pre-planned. It demanded everything I had, but I felt it wrote itself – an exhilarating, exhausting ride. The journal that accompanies it was a steadying, an attempt at control.

Do you read Welsh poetry?
I try to. I read it with difficulty and a dictionary. I'm fond of poems dealing with the spiritual, the numinous. Nature poems. I first started reading them when my son was learning Welsh in school, and he'd have to learn things by heart and I'd go over them with him. I think I read Welsh poetry because it's all around me, but also to see the world from a different perspective. Wales is a small place but reading in Welsh reminds you that its culture is very old, very deep. And there's an informality of address, I think, in Welsh poetry. The poet is simply part of the community and accepted as such. I'm fond of parallel texts: Welsh on one side and English on the other, ideally several translations by

different people. Because the personality and the sensibility of the translator always shapes the way the poem reads. On the whole I'd prefer a plain prose translation, to let the Welsh sounds take over. I read things out loud, in a rather imperfect way, to get a sense of the musicality of it.

The voices of your speakers often sound very like you, but you've also adopted the voices of very obviously different people, including men - I try to write in a speaking voice, to use relatively plain language. I do adopt the voices of other people, yes, men too. But of course! Isn't it a shame that we only have one life? Imagination opens doors into other existences. What I like best about writing poetry, I think, is extending my own experience into that of an owl or spider or something. But the I of 'Cometary Phases' is completely me, without disguise: as full-time teacher, full-time mother, carer. That's my life. The 'I' of 'Burning the Candle' is more the writing me. The fringe context is suggested in the journal. I have been asked whether I use the third person as a way of evasion or disguise but I've rarely done this deliberately. Many of my poems deal with that dilemma of needing distance and closeness that all writers have to try and balance: the need to give yourself to the work with consideration for the family. It may be worse for women. Writing in the third person can release things that are difficult or too close to write about but I don't think I do that very much.

A good many of your poems are openly woman-centred; you often write with an identifiably female voice. Would you identify yourself as a feminist? I wouldn't identify myself as a feminist. I write about female experience because that's what I've got. I'm very happy as a woman. I can imagine myself as a man. I hope all writers can (or try). I don't think I've needed to be a feminist. I've been very fortunate. I think men's and women's roles are different and I've been able to negotiate my role quite satisfactorily.

Do you think your gender has had any effect on your practice?

My practice has certainly been affected by the fact of my gender but to some extent I've been able to hide inside my roles as teacher, housewife, mother. I live and write in an environment that is uneasy with artistic expression. I'm part of a community of very practical people who don't always see the need for it. But I don't see that as a man I'd have had an easier time in this community. Until I took early retirement to look after my mother-in-law I'd always earned my own living. When I was a full-time mother, we had the small-holding and I did lots of work on that. I grew up very much in a working class environment, in a family where reading was a waste of time; it had to be kept secret. My mother wouldn't have encouraged writing. My father in law had tremendous respect for the word and the number, but as tools. (People like Brenda Chamberlain and other artists were never seen as equals within the community. Their work wasn't seen as making anything happen.)

So I have a sort of shame about writing. I hide it. I have tried not to write, partly out of feeling that a complete life should be lived, and partly because it causes problems within the family. For several years I gave it up. Poem after poem actually describes this conflict, I think now. In 'Latency', I'm trying to kill off the writer within me; 'In Women's Thanatological' (*Cometary Phases*) is about how it might be easier to neutralise the imagination than live with the itch to write and the frustration of not being able to. But male writers must feel this as well...

Does gender seem as important as ever to you today?
Gender is important to me because I have a woman's body and the body is where we live. To go back, 'Bonanza' deals with R.S. Thomas telling me more or less that what I thought about as a young woman was of no interest. It wasn't poetic enough. I would object to that. And when I did start writing, well, that poem is defiance isn't it? It says 'look, wringing out nappies and gardening is just as much subject for poetry as walking along the beach as a middle-aged vicar.'

You have written poems about other women writers, Brontes and

Sylvia Plath...

It isn't the poetry of the Brontes that appeals to me. My affinity with Dorothy Wordsworth has to do with her methods of observation, the quietness and withdrawnness of her life. Plath I find inspiring because of her use of language and threatening because of her flirting with death. I have to be careful about Plath; as Anne Stevenson said, 'she sits like a black crow on all our shoulders'. I've found American women writers very important. I read Emily Dickinson a lot but people like Anne Rouse, lately Ellen Hinsey who writes long meditative poems, and the Native American Joy Harjo's voice is very strong. Some of Margaret Atwood's earlier poetry was very important.

What about poets associated with Wales, say, Brenda Chamberlain?

Brenda Chamberlain's work I know of course because of her geographical connection with this area but I find much of her poetry, especially in *The Green Heart*, forced, too ornate. Only a few speak to me directly, like 'The Islandman' (written before she lived on Bardsey). But that doesn't mean I'm not influenced by her. I like Alison Bielski's earlier work, the freedom of her forms and the clarity of her images.

And your own generation?

If I had to take only one to a desert island, it would be Anne Stevenson. I love her different voices. And the formal control and compassion that she brings to the speaking voice. Her short poems are brilliant. I have most of her collections. I'm biased towards contemporary novels by women, but many of the poets I read are male. Of my own generation, I'd never known anybody else who wrote to be published until I met Gillian Clarke, when we were developing a creative writing option for the A level. I remember finding her poem 'Babysitting' after I'd submitted my first collection: I was instantly jealous, because that was how I was trying to write. So Gillian's work I enjoy and admire. Gwyneth Lewis but she is much younger. Sheenagh Pugh is a very clever poet; I very much liked her sequence 'Earth Studies' and I envy her range. I used to look out for Jean Earle's work, while Glenda Beagan's poetry has a wise intensity that deserves more recognition. I'm very fond of Dannie Abse's early work, Tony Curtis and David Constantine. On my shelf I can see Paul Henry, Chris Meredith, John Barnie but more of the writers are canonical, the English greats, the Irish – Heaney – and the Americans of course.

Do you think of yourself as a Welsh writer?
To be honest I don't really see myself as writing from within any community of poets, whether women, Wales-based or any other. It isn't relevant to the way I live and the way I write. I write as I do because I am a woman and because I live where I do.

Do you think of Bardsey – Enlli – as part of Wales? Or somehow separate?
Well Bardsey's a strange place. It's had two languages for almost two centuries, because of the lighthouse and the lighthouse families who came from all over Britain. The lighthouse was built by Cornish stonemasons at a time when the island would have been almost exclusively Welsh-speaking. But Bardsey is geographically a part of Wales, an enriched part.

Is it possible to say what Wales is to you?
I'd say that coming to Wales helped me to develop a stronger sense of self. I don't identify myself as Welsh. I'm very proud that one side of my family is Welsh but it's not a qualification. One of the biggest satisfactions of my life has been learning Welsh and being able to read some of the literature. But I don't think it matters whether people think of me as Welsh or not. I think what Wales did more than anything else, apart from making me feel at home, was give me a sense of otherness. How do you define your sense of self unless you have something to measure it by? I wasn't encouraged to learn Welsh for a long time. Things are different now, but then it gave me that sense of isolation, of being other, that I think writers need. I think writers need to spend time alone, to be aware of their own separate identity and perhaps living in Wales has emphasised that. I think if I moved away from this

area, (the relentlessness of the sea does get irksome), it would be somewhere in Wales

Do you think living in Wales – on Bardsey – has affected your sense of your craft?
I'm not sure. The same resources are open to all of us. I have shelves of books in English and Welsh that I can read and learn from. Living every day with another language has enriched my vocabulary as well as my experience. In *Burning the Candle*, although eyes, like the candle, are a key image, it wasn't until quite late on and seemingly by accident that I realized that the Welsh for the pupil of the eyes is *cannwyll llygaid*, the candle of the eye. I wouldn't have had that. How can awareness of two cultures not enrich? Bardsey's important but it's just one of the places, one of the landscapes, I write about. It's somewhere I've spent a lot of time; it's in my psyche. I wonder how I'd be different if I had never come to Wales. It's almost impossible to tell. In all our lives there are many possible paths, roads not taken. I might never have been a published writer. Or written novels. I often write about other people's stories. Heartbreaking stories. What do you do with heartbreak? Let it break your heart or make something with it? I try and make something out of it.

Thank you very much, Christine.

CATHERINE FISHER

Catherine Fisher has published three volumes of poetry with Seren: *Immrama* (1988), *The Unexplored Ocean* (2000) and *Altered States* (2003), in addition to a pamphlet *Folklore* (Smith/Doorstop Books, 2006). She is also a prolific novelist, known for award-winning works of fiction for young adults including the trilogies *The Snow-Walker* and *The Oracle*, and *The Book of the Crow* quartet. She lives in Newport.

Perhaps we could begin with Wales: do you think of yourself as a Welsh writer? What is it that Wales offers you as a writer?
For me Wales is a series of places. Specifically it's the local landscape: the actual hills and forests. If I think of Wales that's what I think of: I don't think of a political entity or a cultural entity, really, or a linguistic one. I think of actual local places.

And those places are invariably Gwent.
Usually, yes, because it's the place I know best.

How do you get at the Gwent landscape? Do you go there?
Oh I go there. I walk all over it. And explore it. And have done for many years. And I read about it and try and soak myself in it, really.

Do you have a favourite place in Gwent? (And why?)
Grey Hill. Wentwood. Caerleon. Places with a strong literary or historical feel. Caerleon is important in Roman history and has strong Arthurian connections. Grey Hill is a focal point in the

landscape, with a stone circle and views down the estuary.

It's quite a sinister landscape at times isn't it?
Very scary. Yes. The Levels are very different, really, from
anywhere else. Very flat, very marshy. At night as you say they're
very ghostly. The Severn, as well, the river itself, is a very powerful thing.

Why?
Because it's tidal. That huge bulk of water moves up and down
the estuary like a sort of breathing and it controls everything: it
controls the climate and the communications into Gwent, the
bridges and so on, and it controls the history of the place; it's just
always there. And I live very near the river Usk, which is a tribu-
tary of the Severn, so the river is always a presence

*It's got that huge tidal range as well. So you're either looking at river
or mud.*
Yes exactly. That physicality is what really interests me. Wales is
too big to think about in total. I think about places that I know.

*Can you say any more about that physicality? How and why do you
find it interesting?*
I like to try and reproduce physical details in poems. What things
feel like, textures, mud, cold, rain, small details. They can say
everything.

*Do you find language does that for you? That words can make things
– real things – available? That language is reliable – does what you
ask of it in that way?*
Language can recreate some sort of image in the reader's mind,
but that is limited. So there are many times it doesn't work but
the obsession is in keeping on trying.

Do you find writing hard work? Pleasurable? Both?
Both in equal measure. But the pleasure comes from the work.

History is a powerful presence in your poetry, partly perhaps because of your own quite complex historical relationship with Wales, but so are fantasy and myth. How do you like to understand the relationship between history and myth in Wales? Can they be differentiated?
I think they're fused really. I've always been interested in myth and legend, and I think that's because a lot of it again comes out of the landscape and is inherent in the landscape. I like to place my stories where I think they belong, or to see what stories a place suggests.

What do you mean?
My novel *The Candleman*, which is a children's novel set on The Levels, is an example of a story like that. It's about the implacable indifference of the river and was totally suggested by that place and what's happened there.

When did you start to be interested in myth and legend?
It's hard to remember. The Arthurian legend attracted me early. Also I read a lot of folktales.

Do you have a favourite myth, or perhaps myth cycle, today?
I love the Norse stuff, Viking, Icelandic. So I read a lot of it, and I have friends who are storytellers. But I've got a big collection of books on early Welsh literature. It's usually Welsh. I'm fascinated by the Welsh Triads. They're basically a set of memoranda for lost stories. So you've just got the suggestion of a story and the whole story that was there has gone. (I use Rachel Bromwich's University of Wales edition, which has great footnotes.[1]) Because here is a sort of aide-memoire for a medieval story-teller; a set of outlines of which they would have known the infill but which we no longer have; so a novelist or poet can just put anything they like on them. But they're evocative enough to draw that out.

And are you the sort of reader who needs to know the original?
Yes. I go as far back as possible. Until the language changes.

So can you read any of the originals?

I read Welsh quite well. I learned it as a second language.

Why do we need myth do you think?
I don't know. That's a very difficult question. I think we need
stories: we can't live without stories because we're always trying
to get ourselves to the truth, and myth is about the truth in
pictures or in images. But myths aren't static either. If they're
static they're dead. The ones that are still alive are still being
reworked constantly, like the Grail story. That story is still very
much alive. Tolkien said myths are lies breathed through silver.
They're true but they're not literally true.

What do you want me to take from your myth? Your myth-making?
I don't know. I think I use it more in fiction than in poetry. I think
I'd just like people to read the poems and feel teased by them, feel
excited by the language and the imagery and want to go away
and think about where they came from, and find out a bit more
about them.

*Which returns us to your Wales. I'm always struck by the number of
place names in your poems. Some of your contemporaries consciously
avoid citing the names of places they write about. In your poetry,
though, place-names seem somehow to acquire a kind of poetic nature
in and of themselves.*
Well I don't take the *name* of the place. I take the place. And if I
write about the place then obviously I'll use the name. You use the
name often as a, well, like a spell in a sense, an evocation. To
summon up the place and also to summon up an idea of the
place for someone who hasn't been there. If you've never been
there and you don't know what the word means it's just a sound,
but very often in the sound you can hope people conjure some
idea of what the place is like. Do you know David Jones' poem
'The Sleeping Lord'? He has a long list in one part of the poem
of the rivers of South Wales, and he chants them like...

An incantation.
Yes: an incantation. It's fantastic. Wonderful. And the names

summon up some sort of magic, which I really like. I try and do the same sort of thing.

So if Wales is magic...
Ah. [*Laughs.*] But you have to be careful now. This is the thing that comes up all the time in children's fiction about Wales. It's always the magic place to which English children go on holiday and have strange adventures... and that's difficult. Wales is a real place. But then I don't think myth and reality are opposites. They're just different ways of looking at the same place, or event.

When you write about real people, they are often historical aren't they? In some ways you seem to like holding the contemporary culture of Wales at a bit of a distance.
I don't know; I mean, I live in Wales now. I just write about things that interest me and that I like. I suppose the span of what's in the books tells you that. I like historical things, I like fiction, I like fantasy and I like mythology.

And Wales accommodates all those things.
Yes. It does have all those things. The contemporary you see all around you, every day. It's always there; it's always in your face, in a sense. But I like to look for other things. Things that you just see out of the corner of your eye or you see going past in the train or you don't quite see.

Why do you think you particularly like 'historical' things, and the 'things you don't quite see'?
It's about re-fingering them. It's about re-holding them. Getting in touch with them again.

What for?
With the estuary poems, it is a form of chronicling. But most poems are just adventures in language. They're playing with language, playing with images, trying to find a way of getting that idea, or that information or that event, down in the most beautiful and precise and eloquent way possible. When you've done

that you can sort of sit back and say, it works, or it doesn't work. When you feel it does work then you think, well, it's got to go out there now.

It seems a bit as if you think there's been some kind of disconnection between the contemporary – our 'now' – and that world, and when it 'works' you're keeping the connections open...
Well it's very easy to be swallowed up in the modern contemporary world isn't it? And yes, I think poets do have to do that: they have to take things and say look at this again. Look at that again.

I was going to ask you about the role of the poet. It seems to bring with it a particular duty –
Yes. I think the poet's duty is to pay attention to the things that interests him or her and to – well, stop everything and say look: *look – at – that!* That's what a poem does, isn't it? It's very small. It puts things in front of you; it says, look at that time, or that place or that object.

Magnifies.
Magnifies it. And you have to stop and you have to read the poem. You have to read a poem in a certain way; you can't just gallop through it. It makes you stop and concentrate on that little moment, whatever it was.

Do you think of the poet as being effectively male?
No. I don't think of the poet as having a gender, really. In fact I don't think of the poet at all. I just think of me [*laughs*].

The influences you've cited, Keats, Donne, Edward Thomas, David Jones...
But that's because of history; women didn't have the chance to publish and be heard. So there aren't many women poets. But I don't like those writers because they're male or female; I don't even consider that. I just like the poems that they write. Actually I don't necessarily like those writers in particular. I don't know much about them. It's just the poems.

*What about your own generation? Are you conscious of working
within a kind of community which is Welsh?*
Yes I am.

Who do you feel you connect with in that community?
There are lots of people at the moment: Sheenagh Pugh for one.
Hilary Llewellyn Williams I think is a really great poet. Gwyneth
Lewis. Gillian Clarke. These are people whose work is obviously
good and you feel connected to it. Paul Henry and Robert
Minhinnick. But I don't think I have a sense of literary commu-
nity really. The writers I mentioned are probably the ones I
admire most in Wales. And R.S. Thomas of course.

You like RS?
Yes. Yes. Very much. He's very austere; very remote. But I enjoy
the pared-downness of his work. Another poet that I really
admired was George Mackay Brown. For a lot of the same
reasons. He rarely left Orkney, I believe, and really celebrated that
place.

*I think I'd say that both of those writers approach things in quite
similar ways to you. They both ground mythology in an earthy reality;
they uncover, open it up. You use archaeology to do something a bit
similar: the earth represents the here and now – and you go down into
or through it...*
That's right: you burrow down into it and you find certain things
that interest you. Yes. I worked as an archaeologist for a while. It's
a very physical thing to do, and you have long hours when your
mind is empty. You're not reading; you're just digging or
whatever, and you're intimately involved with the textures of the
soil and the mud, and the weather. Working indoors you don't
need to worry about the weather. But if you work outdoors the
weather forecast is the thing you watch all the time. So it was
great for poetry: there was so much to write about.

*Some of those archaeological poems are quite ghostly, aren't they?
Their inhabitants seem otherworldly. Like the woman in your poem*

about the cromlech; not sinister exactly but certainly other.
Sometimes I write a poem and when it's finished it's so different
to whatever I had at the beginning that... well, you just don't
know what it is. You just put it on the page and put it out there.
You just have to say: 'make of it what you will because I don't
know what happened to it or what it's become'.

You didn't know how that one would end up?
No. I had no idea... It came from a visit I made to a tomb in
Anglesey. I'm not sure what it becomes in the end, even if it
becomes anything.

*Do your poems always take shape in the same way? Do you revise
much?*
Poems usually start with a line, or an idea. The best ones start
with a line. But sometimes this doesn't make it to the final draft
– it was a trigger. Sometimes you have to excavate a lot of stuff
before you reach the 'poetry' layer. It lies very deep and is hard
to find. Poems take a long time. I tend to come back to them over
weeks and months, and re-edit. I have written to commission but
I don't feel these are the most successful poems, unless by happy
accident.

*You seem very conscious of the sea as a presence, and as an influence
on the landscapes you write about. The sea seems to open up Wales,
your Wales.*
Well I suppose the sea was the way to travel the country
especially from north to south, because the interior is so
mountainous. Yes: the sea, the coast, the estuary and the rivers I
find really interesting. And again that's a textural thing. The mud
and the colours of the mud. When I was writing *The Candleman*,
I once spent a whole day just sitting on the sea wall at Gold Cliff
looking at the estuary and the colours of the estuary and the
sand. And you really realise that, although it just seems a flat
expanse of mud, it is constantly changing; the way the light, the
sand, the smell all change is fascinating...

Is it also a dimensional thing? Are you drawn by the way it merges land and sea?
It's very much a liminal place, where there is no edge. Yes. I've done some new poems about that. It's just a sort of a place where there are no borders... it is a border but there are no boundaries. As you say, where does the sea begin? And where does the land end?

One of the things it does in your poems is widen or expand 'Wales', as it were, to admit Ireland. Can you tell me a bit about your own connections with Ireland?
My family came from Ireland in the 1840s together with most of Newport and Cardiff. They were from Cork, Waterford. The bottom southwest corner. Not near Wales.

Why did they leave their homes? Were they driven out?
They came over in the Famine. Of course there were stories, family stories, about it. People from the same area stuck together I suppose; anyway they all ended up in Newport, the part of Newport called Pillgwenlly which is the docks area now. It's right on the estuary: they came ashore and they didn't move any further, they sort of encamped themselves. So it was very much an Irish settlement apart from Newport, a quarter of a mile away from Newport; it established itself there as a colony.

How did you find out what happened?
I can't remember where I got it from. I've just always known it. It's that sort of place and community. I suppose I got to a point when I wanted to write about it. I don't know whether it started from writing about my family history, which I'd been researching, or from writing about the estuary; those two things just merged together in the poems. I think probably the family history set it off.

When you say your family, was that both sides, maternal and paternal? Were your ancestors already married, or did two separate strands of the family land up there at the same time?

Six of my great-grandparents were from Ireland and from the same area. The others were from Wales and from the West Country.

And they converged in Newport.
Yes. Everyone intermarried: it was a very close community. They weren't allowed to marry outside their faith, so they all intermarried. But when I was researching the family, I did look up some old stuff: newspaper accounts of the time. And there's a very strong feeling of, well, prejudice I suppose, in the community of the time against the Irish incomers. It must have been very difficult for them to live. Very very hostile.

Hostile on grounds of religion presumably...
Well Wales was a very puritan country. It was not accommodating. And there were racial tensions too I'm sure.

And socio-economic hardship. How did they make their living? The docks?
Yes, navvying. Most of my ancestors worked on the docks. So it must have been very, very difficult.

And were the stories themselves mythologised in the family or did you have to work at trying to imagine it?
I imagined a lot of it, I have to say. I mean there are stories. But I just let my imagination go...

Do you think you are writing out of that culture? Or are you writing back into it, wanting to remake it, even re-mould it...
Yes. You don't want it just to vanish. You don't want it to dissipate into the culture around it without having left a mark. So that you can say you know this is what it was like and this is something of what it was like.

And that's not really about you – Catherine Fisher – about inscribing you, your voice, on Wales. It's more about inscribing that mix.

I suppose it's another facet of what the poet does, isn't it? Records something of their society, of their past. Revives it, but also holds it in being. 'This will not die because I've written it down.' It probably will die, but there you are.

So is there a certain sort of anxiety which comes with that sense of what you're up to?
Yes. It's more of a commemoration. But you don't think of any of that when you're writing the poems. You just write it because you fancy writing about that. All the rest of it comes after.

And what about you? Have you always written? Did you start at school or did it take longer for you to think of yourself as 'being' a writer?
I have always written, yes, starting in school. I always seem to have known that's what I would do.

And you also paint, don't you?
I draw. Not pencil, chalk. I do a life class once a week. I love pastels and all the chalky blurred stuff. I do like textures, I have to say. I've been doing that for about 7 or 8 years I suppose.

Do you find that kind of activity feeds into a kind of poetic productiveness? Or frees your mind in the way that digging does?
It doesn't fit into poetry because it's a different kind of concentration. You're concentrating on things which are not words. They're just lines, so you don't think about words at all: you just think about shape and tone and so on. But I do find that I'm writing more poems about drawing, about art. There are quite a few about this process of trying to capture what's there on paper. That's always fascinated me.

David Jones was also an artist wasn't he? When did you come across him? I mean you came across Keats and Donne presumably early.
I came across Keats very early. Yes. I read Donne in the sixth form. But I came across Jones because of 'The Sleeping Lord'. That poem is a fragment really, about the Welsh landscape. He

compares the landscape to a man, a lord, asleep: an Arthurian figure. I found it in some anthology or other and really liked it. And then I went on to look at his other work, 'In Parenthesis' and 'The Anathemata' and of course he was a Catholic poet. He was very much into that, into Welsh mythology, and Roman history, as well as his experiences in the First World War and he manages to mesh them altogether. Fascinating. But I wouldn't say that he's influenced me in the way I write because he writes in a very different way.

Do you read Irish writers? It seems to me that Seamus Heaney is not so far from what you do...
Yes Heaney is probably the one I read the most. He was a great poet. And lately I've become very keen on Yeats, who I think was an extraordinary poet.

Have you got new work coming out, or have you sent anything off recently?
I have a lot of poems waiting to be sorted into a new collection. At the moment I'm concentrating on the fiction – I'm working on a four book Young Adult set called *The Chronoptika*. Book One, *The Obsidian Mirror*, and Book Two, *The Box of Red Brocade*, are already published. I'm working on the third volume now.

How does writing the children's fiction affect your poetry? Do you have two different heads? Or do they co-exist happily?
They don't co-exist at all. They fight it out. You can't write poetry when you're writing a novel. Or I can't anyway. Because the rhythms of the words are wrong so if you do try to write poetry it comes out in a very prosy fashion.

So why do you turn to the poem to express something? What is it about the poem? It's a very different genre. When I'm teaching I often equate the poem with a painting.
It is in a sense like a drawing. It's something you can home in on and pare down so that you end up with something very small. Whereas the novel is the opposite: it's always growing. You're

always feeling your way through a novel. As if you're going along a road. You're trying to find the end of it. With the poem it's totally different.

And yet you've said more than once that narrative is something that turns you on. Is this why you like writing sequences?
I like sequences because it's very hard sometimes to find the subject for a poem. You want to write a poem but you don't know what it's about and the sequence pulls you in a little bit so you've got a bit of room and space to feel your way through it. Sometimes if you can't do that you write a poem and you know that it isn't the one, so you write another. You go through it until you come to what you're actually after.

So it frees you of the coherence of a straightforward narrative?
Yes. It fragments it. You do facets of the narrative. Which is an interesting way of doing it but I can't write poetry when I'm writing a book. You need space to write poetry: or I need a lot of space around me.

Do you remember when you first wrote a sequence? Did you have any kind of sense of it having happened in that way? Or did you collect some things together into a sequence?
The Noah set in *Immrama* was the first sequence I think I ever wrote. I can't remember how that happened. I think I just wrote a poem where I tried to interpret that legend in a contemporary situation and then thought, well how many ways can you do this? Is there more in it? *Immrama* is a category of story: they were always stories about voyaging between islands – that's very much what that book is interested in. I liked the word and it fitted with the book.

Altered States *opens with an epigraph in what I understand is old Irish. What do the words mean and where are they from?*
That epigraph is a stanza describing an exile looking back on an Ireland they will never see again, as they sail away. I didn't translate it because I like mystery – there might be one interested

reader who will track it down.

Would you like people to know you more as a poet, not only as a writer of children's fiction?
I'd like them to know the poems. But I am not the poems and the poems are not me. And neither are the novels me. So I don't particularly want them to know me: it's the poems I want them to know. People often think you give yourself away in your poems but you don't. The poems are a construct which you build like an architect builds a building. There's always something of me in what I've built but a lot of it is about practicalities. The same is true of a poem.

You do it because you can?
You do it because you have to do it. You have to do it. It's an urge, an instinct, an addiction.

And it's not returning to you. It's reaching away from you; it's reaching out into those other terrains.
You make the ball and you roll it off and it rolls away and someone else plays with it and you're busy making another one.

You're not running after it.
No you're not. You're not even noticing where it goes.

Thank you, Catherine.

7. Rachel Bromwich, ed. *Trioedd Ynys Prydein / The Welsh Triads*. Cardiff: University of Wales Press, 1961.

GWYNETH LEWIS

Gwyneth Lewis is the author of six collections of English-language poetry, all published by Bloodaxe: *Parables and Faxes* (1995), *Zero Gravity* (1998), *The Language Murderer* (2000), *Keeping Mum* (2004), *Chaotic Angels* (2005), *A Hospital Odyssey* (2010), and most recently *Sparrow Tree* (2012), winner of the 2012 Welsh Book of the Year Award. A further four have appeared in her native Welsh with Barddas: *Sonedau Redsa a Cherddi Eraill* (1990), *Cyfrif Un ac Un yn Dri* (1996), *Y Llofrudd Iaith* (1999) and *Tair mewn Un* I (2005). Appointed Wales' first National Poet (2005-2006), Lewis was commissioned to produce the bi-lingual poem-window whose six-foot-high letters illumine the upper gallery-space of the Wales Millennium Centre in Cardiff Bay. She has also written several libretti, two plays (a reworking of the Greek tragedy *Clytemnestra* and *Y Storm*, based on *The Tempest*) and a novel (*The Meat Tree: New Stories from the Mabinogion* Seren, 2010). Her non-fiction includes *Sunbathing in the Rain: A Cheerful Book on Depression* (Harper Perennial, 2002) and *Two in a Boat* (Fourth Estate, 2005). She has held fellow-ships at the National Endowment for Science Technology and the Arts, and Harvard, Stanford, Cambridge, Manchester and Swansea Universities.

Can we start by talking about the poets who've been important to your development?
Well in terms of poetic lineage, the people that put me – as the Welsh would say – at the head of my way were largely male. Within the Welsh tradition I learned very early on from male

models, but then I went through a period of not writing, and then went to America in order to start again. All my teachers were men, in fact. Other than Elizabeth Bishop, [Joseph] Brodsky was the main one, [Seamus] Heaney, Derek Walcott... And of course the poetic lineage that they acknowledge, back through W.H. Auden to Robert Frost, Edward Thomas. Very male-oriented. I have to say, the longer I continue, the more I question many aspects of this: I'm rebelling more as I become older!

That's not unusual, is it...
No. In fact I'm thinking that there's a broader way of defining the kind of poetics that appeal to you than gender: you could say that this lineage is very craft-based, formalist, purist but committed to the language of the place where you were born and of that being a fundamental part of your health. So even though they look like formalists, all those patterns from Auden and Heaney come out of local accents. So what looks like purism isn't at all: it's local in a way which has always appealed to me because it allows you to honour the very local with the international at the same time.

So how does that work, exactly?
It seems to me that the trick of writing out of your own language or idiom without being parochial is to use the material you find at your feet but exercising the highest aesthetic standards. Like Cavafy or Pessoa, say; both poets deeply embedded in their own cultures who pushed their art to be world-class.

You seem more self-conscious in your attitude to your languages than Walcott; you keep things more obviously separate.
Well it's complicated. Walcott was important to me. He was at Columbia Writing Division while I was there. We had Brodsky for one term, Derek for another and also C.K. Williams.

Wow. Huge names! What was it like?
I know. Amazing! It exploded all my ideas. And yet there was a kind of coming home. Brodsky, for example, was someone who took poetry to be an absolute good. I'd always felt unreasonably

passionate about poetry and meeting Joseph made me realize that I wasn't alone in this and that there were good cultural and evolutionary reasons for regarding poetry as one of the summits of human achievement. I suppose I stopped feeling so odd. Walcott took me under his wing for a while. The Arts Council in Wales used to run a scholarship for visiting writers, and he'd spent some time in Wales. So he was familiar with the cultural politics of Wales. And I was facing this agonising decision about which language to write in, and he took the trouble to talk it through with me. And he was the one who said, 'You've got to write in English. You've just got to do it.' And his saying that made me think, well maybe I could break through this emotional impasse. Because he was someone who'd refused to abandon the colonial outpost. He's made his own compromises with Creole and Caribbean languages and his classical English education. Although he's drawn the line in a different place from me.

He's refused to abandon any of it, really, has he? He's always doing both.
Quite. And he completely understood bilingualism, because he told me he'd discovered something that I've discovered myself: that you don't compose in one language or the other, you actually compose in both at the same time, and you even do the rhyme at the same time. In fact whenever I translate my own work I do it extremely quickly, in one go, and it rhymes. Very bizarre. So Walcott was wonderful, extremely good to me.

To go back to lineage...
The lineage goes right back, because Brodsky's mentor had been Anna Akhmatova, and he loved the work of Marina Tsvetaeva. It's a very fertile ground because it allows you to travel and not to travel at the same time. Perfect. With Seamus Heaney of course the antecedents were male there. But discovering Nuala Ní Domhnaill later was a huge help because it gave new impetus to my thinking about my Celtic language.

When did that happen?

I met her in Vienna on a British Council event. She made a stray remark about members of her family who'd refused to speak Gaelic suffering from mental illness. And that made a connection for me, made *Keeping Mum* possible. So there are women in my tradition.

Can we home in on them? Who's there?
Well Sitwell was a huge discovery for me. The precision of her writing is very striking and I'm really puzzled as to why she's been underrated and forgotten. I'm fascinated by her interest in science. I found out that she went to visit Edwin Hubble in the US and that he showed her photographic plates of distant galaxies. And Stevie Smith has been very important. I must have read her work at school, but Walcott made us learn 'Tenuous and Precarious'...

By rote?
Yes. He thought that was a great poem, alongside Meredith or Frost. (He used to make us learn all kinds of stuff.) So I read Smith, from cover to cover. I liked her – I've been thinking about my patterns of likes and dislikes in women poets – because she was a fully female writer but without the domestic, which hasn't been a big subject for me.

I've noticed that.
Well my experience of domesticity is that it's dangerous. Stevie Smith was important for an ambition of voice and a kind of intellectual brightness which gave itself full rein. And it seems to me that she's the equal of any male poet. There's no doubt about that. So in a strange way it's not about gender. It's a spirit of communion, a sphere of influence thing. Plenty of men write about the domestic now. So, they've pushed those frontiers forward. It all depends what you're interested in and the means by which you explore it.

You've talked elsewhere about being caught between your two languages. Not being bilingual, I find that agony almost impossible to

imagine: to use both seems such a neat solution. I know things have changed, but wasn't it obvious?
Not obvious at all. The politics were very different in the late seventies, early eighties. I remember being told by a Welsh speaker in North Wales that I wasn't Welsh because I came from South Wales. That was devastating. On the same visit I was told I couldn't *have* a Muse because I was a Muse, because I was a woman.

But you'd already published, and you were still young...
Yes, but I knew that to be a grown-up poet was another thing altogether. There were unresolved issues and I knew I had to grow up. The thing about the Muse affected me badly for a long time. I felt quite angry about that comment so I'm quite impatient of literal interpretations of the Muse. For Brodsky, the Muse is the voice of the language. Much more useful. It could be from here, or here, or here [*gesturing at herself*]. It doesn't matter where, as long as it's in relation to your body. But at that time, there was a lot of invective about treachery in Wales. For example there was a woman teacher at my school with Nationalist convictions, which I respected, but when I got into Cambridge, she never spoke to me again. It was a quite different atmosphere.

The burning houses...
That was the political context, yes. And the sense of personal attack was very strong. I think that's why I felt I had to remove myself to America, at a safe distance, to make a decision so that it wasn't influenced by fear. I wanted it to be a wholehearted choice. And I got there in the end. But it's only recently that bilingualism has been accepted as a benign condition. It's still regarded in some quarters as a betrayal of the Welsh language, because immediately you enter into a relationship with the English, it's taking the place of the Welsh. I dispute that model, because it doesn't work that way in poetry, for me certainly. It seems to me that linguistic inventiveness is stimulated by the rubbing-together of two languages. The more you do of both the better. I get more out of the permissive attitude; a more exclusive

strategy would make me self-conscious, inhibited. It's two models of social order if you like, and I favour a kind of benign anarchy rather than prescriptiveness. But that's at a level of creativity, of course. You can't translate that into politics directly.

But, aesthetically, don't you risk ending up with incoherence?
Yes.

How do you avoid that? Or are things the richer for the anarchy, the untidinesses?
Perhaps this is one reason why I'm a formal poet. Rhyme and metre are centripetal forces and prevent very disparate material from flying apart. But I'm not afraid of chaos; I feel that one of the things that distinguishes artists from other people is their tolerance of disorder before it falls into place artistically.

Is it hard, working in the two languages?
Well one sticking point is that your basic metrical rhythm in English is iambic and in Welsh it's trochaic. So I have trouble writing bi-lingual libretti, because how on earth do you get a Welsh sound to go on top of an English sound when they are fundamentally different? That's the kind of corner you get in.

I can't imagine how you resolve that...
Both feet are mirror images of each other. They're the same stitch but in reverse, like plain and purl. For me both languages are the same, even though they look quite separate. They're part of a larger language. As I've said before [*Guardian* 18th November 2006] as a child, you don't realise that not everyone in the world comprehends both the languages you speak. You think: I understand it, why doesn't the world understand it?'

But you found a cultural place for yourself, and the poetry. If a slightly unusual one.
People tend to say, 'what you're doing is anomalous'. But it seems to me entirely normal. And accidental. I guess if I spoke Swahili and English I'd do the same. The job isn't one of cultural loyalty;

it's a question of artistic loyalty. That's different.

It's more abstract?
Yes, but it's complicated: it has to do with how your poetic composition links to the body. I read in Welsh in Orkney, at the St Magnus Festival, one year, and afterwards Sally Beamish, the composer, said: 'That one was clearly your first language, because your voice is quite different!' The timbre of my voice is much more relaxed, much deeper in Welsh. It was interesting that a musician could hear in the pitch of my voice that I'm more comfortable in Welsh even though I'm very fluent in English.

Welsh-speakers often seem anxious about how their language-use will be judged by other Welsh-speakers –
Well because Welsh is not as standardised as English, there are whole groups of Welsh-speakers who feel that their language isn't good enough. In fact their Welsh is perfectly delicious but they don't consider it so. And there is huge pressure to standardise it and to have it 'pure'; for example the main Eisteddfod contest demands linguistic accuracy. It's quite easy to get your Welsh wrong because of all the mutations. And sometimes very good poems have been dismissed because they've not been grammatically correct, despite being better poems than the more 'academic' ones.

But you're contesting that inclination, by insisting on that inclusivity we were discussing?
Well yes, but I still make sure, as far as I can, that my Welsh is correct! I don't want to give anyone the excuse that they can't read this... But I'm not a purist linguistically. In fact my editor has said to me, 'That's not a correct word' and I say I don't care, that's how my family speaks. But to go back to the whole idea of Wales: there are very acute pressures which aren't immediately visible to people on the outside. With small communities, if there's a very strong feeling of belonging, there's an equally strong feeling of not belonging. I suppose I always want to question where that line is drawn.

You have to draw lines, as a poet, don't you?
Well, I've drawn my own. I don't draw them for other people. I
hate it when lines are drawn by people for others. I don't think
that's right. I'm not the kind of person to conform. I'm not a
gang-joiner.

Are you Chapel?
I was brought up Methodist, but I've gone to Church in Wales.
But I'm not a crowd follower by instinct.

*I'm wondering about politics. You don't seem to have talked very much
about political issues. I'm assuming you were in favour of devolution?*
Politics and current affairs are an enduring interest. When I lived
in New York I was a correspondent for Radio Cymru, so I
regularly used to phone in news reports. I've read newspapers
voraciously ever since I was an undergraduate, my doctorate was
on the politics of literary forgery in the eighteenth century and
my first job in television was researching Current Affairs
programmes. I'm also fascinated by how politics and art go
together. My favourite poet is still Milton. He was a propagandist
for the Cromwell government and thought out his artistic ideas
while he was doing that work. I don't see how you can understand or use language without appreciating the pressures placed
by history and politics on what sounds 'natural' to us. Learning
this is part of being free to act in ways that aren't conditioned by
what other people want you to do. But I'm not a party-political
animal. No one party matches the full spectrum of my convictions – if anything, they're anarchist. I feel that my voting habits
are nobody's business but my own. But yes, I voted for devolution and I feel strongly about it, although I think it's going to take
a generation to come into its own.

*Milton – I don't know why that should seem a surprise but it does.
Tell me more...*
The first thing I loved was the lushness of his vocabulary and his
long, long sentences moving subtly over numerous lines. I find
the pace of his story-telling exciting and the fact that he's not

afraid to talk about ideas as part of the myths he's retelling. And they're the biggest ideas: "the ways of God to man". Recently I listened to *Paradise Lost* as an audio book, in a fantastic recording by Anton Lesser. I hadn't realised before how like science fiction it is, nor how funny.

In Wales, the bards made those links between politics and art real. Of course (unlike Milton) your poems don't truck much with ceremony. But you sometimes seem to me to be doing something pretty bard-like, if only in determinedly representing Wales back to itself; making poetry about things like the health service, for example.

There is a larger space in the Welsh public sphere for poetry than in England or the U.S. I'm not a fan of "bardiness" because of its claim to a special status. Poets are only of value in a public way to the extent that they reflect common experiences, even if that's done in an extraordinary way. For me the authority of any public poem comes not from the poet but from what he or she draws from the poetic tradition. I couldn't be less interested in public poems that say how great a particular writer is. The task is to let language speak in the way it wants to. What I do notice is that the public poems I've written are much more perishable than ones I commission from myself.

Lately you've been working on the early Welsh poet Dafydd ap Gwilym. Why him?

Yes, he's a recent enthusiasm. I was put off Dafydd when I was at school. I thought he was just a boring sexist. But with the publication of Dafydd Johnston et al's *Complete Dafydd ap Gwilym* – in Welsh, you can get literal translations into English online – it suddenly became possible to "see" his work in its entirety. I'm drawn by his combination of intellect and lightness, his wit. I find it breathtaking.

As an English-speaker, what do I miss in reading him in translation?

It's almost impossible to get a sense of his verve from translation. The demands of *cynghanedd* mean that his rhythms are so embedded in the Welsh that you either lose his music or the brilliance of his intellect. The closest 'translation' of Dafydd ap Gwilym's spirit isn't, strictly speaking, a translation at all. Dannie Abse has a series of Dafydd poems in his most recent book *Speak, Old Parrot* (2013), and they catch his flirtatiousness – both sexual and poetic – exactly.

I think I read that you were translating him? You make it seem hopeless! (Mind you, Eva Hoffman's brilliant book Lost in Translation *seems to suggest that all experience involves translation, at some level...)*
The difficulty doesn't put me off the task at all, it makes it more interesting! And even more important to attempt it. Eva Hoffman's book is a wonderful description of the complexities of language and identity. It helped me hugely when I found it. I heard her speak in Germany once and stammered out that I was a huge fan when I met her in the ladies, poor woman! But yes I think that even monoglots are struggling with translation all the time; it's fundamental cognitive work.

To go back to that richly linguistic place which stands behind all this, (perhaps one version of what your Bloodaxe lectures call 'Illyria') do you think of Wales as a refuge or departure point? Or is that to over-tidy the complexities?
Well, I think home is where you have to face your greatest fears. Usually you have to travel to face your greatest fears. My own experience was the reverse; all the things that made me travel I had to face in the end anyway. In the seventies there was a kind of Anglo-Welsh poetry that used Welsh place-names in English poetry as a way of evoking particular feelings in the reader. I didn't like that because it actually excluded people who wouldn't have known those places, so I try and use a place-name, when I use one, for a very particular reason. Because I suppose Wales, or Welsh-speaking Wales, has been where I have had to face, most acutely, questions about the nature of language, and how that links into my own psycho-drama. I can't say it more clearly than that.

It's not a landscape, in your mind any more than it is in your poetry?
I don't write about landscape. Well, perhaps I have in fact but they are always psychological landscapes. Always.

Drawn from the outside...
Well, physically, on the body. The whole way that I learnt English was through body parts (but don't be fooled; that's a literary device); I've never been able to do straight landscapes. Because I think we've got such an emotional investment in that outside, perhaps it's always an internal landscape.

It's like that story Sunbathing *tells about you as a child, getting on to the window-ledge, and looking back in through the window. It's not that you're not here, in Wales; it's that you somehow manage to get to a place where you can look back in at yourself, wherever you are.*
It's about coming out of the body. Somebody once said: 'This is a weird thing to say but you go so far out I'm surprised that you don't have difficulty coming back into your body sometimes.' And I think that poetry is very good in that way; metre is very elastic. It's like taking the bungee jump and you know – ooooh – and I've got to come back, and then you come back to it and it pulls you in. Wonderful!

For me lyric sequences work in the same way – each poem is anchored, has its place, but they can all spring in and out of line. Is that what you mean when you say that narrative is a safe place from which to change things?
Every book is a sequence. I construct it like that. It's important to me that there should be a logic from the beginning of a book to the end. The odd poem comes on its own, but the sequence is my kind of pacing.

Why?
Well, the Eisteddfod competition quite often demands a sequence. You'd be set a sequence of 200 lines on the subject of energy or increasing, or whatever. And so you plan it. It's quite a self-conscious thing. I think the first I did was a sequence about

the Philippines – the Redsa poems. It was interesting. You learn how to construct a long poem. It took me years to win [Lewis won the Crown in 2012 for 'Ynys'] but in the meantime I learned how to take pace myself. It's like making a documentary film. The similarities between making a good television programme and writing poetry amaze me. The trick is to get a narrative which you can follow like a thread through a labyrinth, and then hang your metaphorical observations from that line. It's the contrast between the horizontal and vertical which interests me.

And you get glimpses...
I don't always know exactly where I'm going to end up, but I usually know how long it's going to be. I do know what's going to happen, but not consciously. So it's quite an adventure really.

Several of your sequences represent different perspectives, or voices, like the psychiatrist and Miss D in 'Keeping Mum'. So it tells a story but it's also binary?
Yes, back and forth. The safety comes in a kind of... well, artistic logic. Whenever I've got into difficulties with a line, making its sense clearer always improves it. When the narrative line isn't clear and I've tidied up, it's always a better poem for that. That, it seems to me, is a wonderful argument for truth and beauty going together. I think you have to earn clarity; you have to buy it in kind. In fact that's another aspect of poetry that fascinates me: is how you have to put in your time.

What do you mean?
At the start of a poem, day one, you have no idea what it's about. By day two you're thinking it might be about jealousy, and then on day three you realize it's not about my jealousy, it's about another person's jealousy. Three days-worth of not knowing 'til you see it. By weaving that time into the poem and the whole process of discovery, you get some kind of immunity from time, I think. Meter is implicated in it as well: it's your passport through the experience. Meter is a safe form of knowing, and of learning things, in going into dodgy territory.

Do you favour a particular stanza form?
Quite often the difficulty for me is starting – I'm always worried until I know what the stanza is. Once I get that I'm off. So the first couple of lines are quite tricky until I've got my shape. And whenever I try to free it up it gets even more restricted. That's something I'm always thinking about.

You wouldn't vary the form?
[*Laughing*] Derek Walcott used to say 'I'm always terribly suspicious of someone who changes the form in the middle.' And yes – but I think you can set off a number of different voices in different metres against each other. One sequence which really influenced me was Melissa Green's *The Squanicook Eclogues* (1987) (she wrote a wonderful memoir, too) and her models are classical eclogues, idylls. Gertrude Schnackenberg as well. She's a brilliant poet; I learned a lot from her sequences. And I love really long poems. Like James Merrill's *The Changing Light At Andover* (1982).

A Hospital Odyssey *was a bold idea, not least because it seems terribly personal on one level. Was it gruelling to write?*
No, it was exhilarating and joyful. The subject of health was so vast that a long poem felt like a short form in which to consider it. It's the most ambitious poem I've written and the main emotion I felt while writing it was intense anxiety, lest I fail to catch what I'd imagined on paper. It took five years of reading and thinking to prepare to write it.

I know the form was Villon's, but it also reminds me of Byron's Don Juan – *the ruthless deflating effects of his rhyme-scheme, so you grin despite yourself. You do that elsewhere; you wield a mean pun. But it's more wit than clowning, perhaps...*
Yes: when I was deciding which stanza pattern to use, Byron's Don Juan measure was one I considered. It's interesting that you mention Byron. I'm becoming more interested in him as a figure and as a poet. He's certainly a must-read in terms of how to pace a story and how to undermine your own seriousness...

Women have been writing poetry in Wales for centuries, but they're at last getting critical attention. And two out of the three National Poets so far. It's exciting for someone like me, in some ways, but as you were hinting earlier, gender perhaps seems a rather blunt-edged way of thinking about any poetic scene, these days. What do you think? Would you define yourself as a feminist?

Yes I would call myself politically a feminist. I grew up reading Tillie Olsen and Betty Friedan and Kate Millett, all those critics: radical feminism was very much in vogue when I was at university. But artistically I'm not a feminist; because although the gender category is interesting to me and full of anxiety and, therefore, fertile, it's not a frame around the poem. It's like a faultline through the poem. But personally and politically and critically, growing up – and living in Cambridge in the mid-seventies – you couldn't not be aware of feminist theory.

But aesthetically you want to move beyond it.

Well yes because, I think, I want to be my best, I want to be a full woman, or a full poet, in all categories of my existence.

Are you bothered by the thought of being in a book of women poets?

No. I mean, let's try to imagine other different categories. Would I be worried about being in a book about Christian poetry? No. And I think it's important not to be naïve about the cultural politics and power structures involved in publishing and reputation-making and so on. But it's a question of your fundamental drive as an artist. Is it for a good reputation or to be the best poet you can possibly be? The second is my main concern. I wouldn't want to say that gender isn't significant to me because it has everything to do with what I am about physically. I am a woman and my writing comes from, is intimately related to, my body. And the more I go on the more I realise how much that's true in ways I hadn't understood before. What I can do is completely dictated by that. But in terms of subject, the category of gender is not a primary one for me, although I use it, a lot, because it's one of those faultlines of anxiety. Anything that makes you feel a bit uneasy I'll go for. Because it's always fertile. It's a great subject. There's no point in replicating what's been done very well before you. The trick is to put a new spin on it.

Can we talk about poetry as detective fiction? There's so often some crime, some sense of retribution in the air in your work...
I suppose I think there's some cost in everything, that there are always consequences in any approach to anything. It's a big theme. In the end any poet's reputation will rest on the poem itself; but what fascinates me is what you have to do with your life in order to write those poems. There are choices to be made all the time; and I think it makes the difference between writing something that is really pretty good and something that is very good. That's the distinction. It's not actually a question of detection so much as discernment.

Of the genuine – authentic – from the fake or forgery?
Yes. The forgery is always pretty good, but I don't want the forgery. I want the very good thing which is authentic.

What do you actually mean by 'authentic' though? The authenticity of a word, of language in general, or of poetic language specifically?
I mean authentic poetically. I give up a narrow personal meaning, and am led by the poem into a new version. And if the poem is any good, what I have is an even fuller, if indirect, version of my situation. I'm not confessional.

Well as you say the poems play with your voice, your experiences and ideas. They have to. And yet they aren't life-writing. So how are they authentic?
The thesis I wrote on forgery showed that whether you call something a forgery or not is political. If you agreed with the politics of a certain editor, you'd call an eighteenth century ballad a wonderful contribution to learning. But if you disagreed with Macpherson, you'd call Ossian a forgery. In fact Macpherson wasn't doing much different from Bishop Percy. So it's an external label – not one applied by the writer. I think the only judge is your personal life; and every poet has to judge that for him or herself.

Jo Shapcott's always said, why can't I have this fictional 'I'? Novelists are allowed to...
The 'I' is always fictional in poetry. You see, it's all about perform-ance. Poetry is a kind of authentic lie: it's a pretend but it's not a pretend. It's that funny theatrical act. I remember when that poem about learning English first came out – people said: oh that poor girl, she's been abused. NO! I mean CULTURALLY! And I always think, oh dear, my poor father. So it is a performance; but it's a performance where I am being both deadly serious and deadly playful. You have to allow yourself that.

That word 'deadly'... you're not in it for fun.
No. Well, I am and I'm not. Being deadly serious allows you to crack jokes. I do have a hard-edged purpose in mind. I'm not in it to waste my time. It's a form of discernment.

Love, too?
Yes – [*laughing*] don't tell too many people, but I am a love poet. I'm also a political poet but people don't see that because I'm not using politics like a subject. I mean the attack is political, but not party-political. The great thing is not to get co-opted. And to have the courage to remain open-minded about it rather than dogmatic. That's important.

The role of National Poet is often used as a marker of political independence. And of course you were the first. It must have been exciting – but how did you balance the two languages?
The post of National Poet came out of the achievement of devolution, yes; it still seems an exciting and logical embodiment of Wales speaking up for itself. When I took the job, it wasn't obvious at all what being a 'national' poet was. I took it to mean a question of platform, as with writing a poem for the opening of the Senedd or commenting on the Welsh Rugby Union. And I trusted the poetry to look after me. The joy of the role was exploring what I felt needed saying in a public poem – as opposed to a 'Gwyneth Lewis' poem. When I was appointed I decided that the only reason I could possibly do it was because I

believe in poetry and that that would keep me sane. There's a huge distinction between the artistic principles which allow me to write safely, and personality stuff, which is different. I drew the line between them. In fact that element of performance in the poetry helped. It's somewhere where things aren't narrowed to the personal; they're much more open. So your sense of personality is actually expanding rather than contracting. You adopt an 'I' because the poem needs an 'I', but it differs each time.

And it can sometimes feel as if the I is everywhere, in your work, as a result.
It's everywhere. It's odd. I never know where it's going to go. But I've stopped letting it worry me. Even today, if I stay in that space I'm OK. It's not personal; I centre myself with that. It's partly what *Sunbathing in the Rain* is about: if you are able to centre yourself in that tranquillity (whether you're a poet or not) that's your state of health. Joseph Brodsky used to talk about Frost's bird, 'like one who took everything personally'. You mustn't. That's not a wise way to live.

Thank you very much.

WENDY MULFORD

Wendy Mulford founded the influential poetry press, Street Editions in 1971, and published most of the leading lights of that time – Prynne Crozier Oliver Forrest Thompson Raworth and later Denise Riley, in small but fine editions, frequently with artwork by Julia Ball (distinguished East Anglian painter., b. 1930).

In the 90s Street Editions amalgamated with Reality Studios, to become Reality Street co-edited with Ken Edwards, which continued to publish cutting edge work, by Maggie O'Sullivan Denise Riley, Fanny Howe, and the influential anthology soon to be reprised, *Out of Everywhere: linguistically innovative poetry by women from North America & the UK*, ed. O'Sullivan, 1996., reprint 2006; afterword by Wendy Mulford.

Wendy Mulford's *Selected Poems, and suddenly supposing* (Etruscan Books, 2002) contains most of the 13 small-press collections up to that date: including ones by Poetical Histories, Circle Press, Ferry Press, and many others. Her *Nevrazumitelny* (1991) has been set to music by Michael Parsons and performed & recorded by the avant-garde group, the Vocal Constructivists (premiere London 2013.) Her work has been performed across the UK, the US & Europe. Recent commissions include *The Unmaking* (with Michael Parsons) Cork, 2005, and *Cloud Cover Imponderable*, Parasol Gallery, London, 2009, to coincide with the exhibition by Keith Tyson.

Wendy Mulford's most recent work has appeared in a number of online journals and anthologies, including *Yellowfield* from Buffalo, *Molly Bloom*, from East Anglia, and as a reviewer of Luke Elwes' work, the East Anglian online.

Work has also appeared in *The Ground Aslant: an Anthology of Radical Landscaper Poetry*, ed. Harriet Tarlo (Shearsman 2011); *By the North Sea: an anthology of Suffolk Poems*, ed. Aidan Semmens (Shearsman, 2013), and work is due to appear in *EST: Collected Reports from East Anglia* (Dunlin Press, 2015).

Most recent collections since the *Selected Poems* include: the collaborative *Whistling Through the Nightwood* (Orphean Press, 2008), with Anne Beresford, Herbert Lomas and Pauline Stainer, and *The Land Between* (Reality Street, 2009).

In an article published in 1990 you talk about attempting 'to ground my work in the multiple voices of my life.' Do you still think of your writing in these terms?
Well, yes, but actually I'm not the best person to talk about Wendy-Mulford-from-whenever-it-was because I've got such a bad memory. Wendy Mulford had to take a lot of drugs because for a long time, since I was 15, I suffered from epilepsy. The memory gets wiped each time. Everything is gone and you have to start again.

Was it frightening?
It was frightening. It's not something you would ever want or choose. But it's always been me; it's always been absolutely inextricably linked with my creativity. I see it as part of the shaping of the kind of poet I am; the kind of writer, thinker, person that I am. In fact the coming-and-going of memory, and its relationship to my sense of identity, has I think been part of my way of relating to the world. It's certainly connected to the multiple voices, though of course that perspective was culturally prominent when I was teaching in the seventies and eighties.

You're often grouped with poets who are very self-conscious about language but in your work the fracturing is more, as you imply, experiential-seeming.
Yes. It works itself out formally, and is at least partly to do with the kind of opportunities that surroundings and contexts suggest.

Can we talk about surroundings and contexts? You started your writing life in Cambridge and you work out of Suffolk, where you still live. But you were raised in Wales, and that's remained important for you, hasn't it?

Absolutely: the sense of connection with Wales has remained constant. Sometimes it's been more prominent but it's always been there. The only family that I know about, that I can identify (because I don't know on my father's side) is my mother's family. Three generations of my maternal family are buried in Llanfihangel Crucorney churchyard on the edge of the Black Mountains. I grew up and went to school in Wales, and my mother lived in Usk until she died in the early eighties; I inherited the family home. So a large part of my family story is there. I came east to university, to Cambridge, in the early sixties; and though I stayed in East Anglia, we returned to Wales as often as we could, to our families. The sense of Wales as the imaginary is another thing. That's ebbed and flowed.

You were quite young when you went to Cambridge. Did you miss Wales?

Well I was very inexperienced. And I was going back every holidays to my parents and a life in Monmouthshire much like that which I had lived before. A lot of my friends were returning: we hadn't escaped at that stage although a lot of us did eventually.

Were you conscious of wanting to escape?

No. Cambridge had family connections. In fact I was continuing a family tradition except that I was the first girl to get a higher education – in the teeth of family opposition. And I could read Archaeology and Anthropology there which was what I wanted. But I wasn't happy actually. I felt very inadequately prepared beside friends who had been at independent schools. I simply didn't know anything compared to them, in so many ways, culturally.

Did you think of coming back to Wales?

By the time John James and I were together, we were in our late

twenties and had children to support. Our work was in
Cambridge, and for me in London at Thames Polytechnic where
I was lecturing. And Cambridge was a very stimulating context,
at that time. I mean they were having the anti-university sit-ins at
Kings in 1968 and that was very lively.

*Poetically of course it was about the liveliest place you could have
found.*
Oh yes; that was how John and I met. But I didn't know anything
about that scene. I didn't even know it existed.

So what were you doing? How did you come into contact?
I had begun a research project on John Clare's later poems

Clare seems an interesting choice.
Well I found myself in profound sympathy with what he was
writing in connection with the natural world. It seemed to me that
unlike the great romantics, he actually saw things for what they
were. I was looking at those really bleak nature poems he wrote
before he went completely off the rails in the 1830s. In those days,
you were allowed to handle the manuscripts; you could even
borrow them. I read a lot of the poem-drafts in manuscript, and
all the letters in the British Museum between Clare and his
genteel patrons. My thesis was about the way the poems had been
interfered with and how Clare freed himself from all that.
Anyway, I started writing myself under the influence of Clare,
and sent what I'd written to Donald Davie because he'd been
lecturing at Cambridge and I had respected him. He was at Essex
where Andrew Crozier was one of his graduate students, and
Davie passed my stuff on to Andrew. And being very energetic
and full of curiosity about other writers, Andrew came to my
house in Cambridge with a bunch of other poets including John
James, John Hall and Tim Longville. I was teaching English and
Drama in a secondary school at the time. They invited me to the
pub, The Panton Arms, down the street from where Jeremy
(Mulford) and I were living. And I began going to the gatherings
of poets in Jeremy Prynne's rooms in Gonville and Caius.

And your press, Street Editions, came out of your involvement with that group?
Well we were doing it all the time. *The English Intelligencer* was being wound out on the Gestetner and John James had been doing *The Resuscitator*. And when my aunt died and left me a small amount of money I decided to start my own press, and published everyone I knew – J.H. Prynne, Andrew Crozier, John James, Douglas Oliver, later Tom Raworth, Denise Riley, Veronica Forrest-Thomson. Much later I joined up with Ken Edwards' Reality Studios; he still runs it as Reality Street. My involvement in publishing was 1972-1998. Twenty-five years...

In a sense Cambridge was where your identity as a writer took root.
It looks like that in the histories. And it's true that Cambridge was influential and enabling for me. Very. But it was also a struggle at first. Other women just weren't around in Cambridge to begin with – Elaine Feinstein had been but she didn't join in with this group around Prynne. It wasn't until I met Denise Riley that I began to have a sense of what could be, if the politics of the whole poetry scene in the mid to late 60s were different. Being a woman and a poet of the kind I was – I leave the labels to you – wasn't easy.

Was this the same time that you were active in the Trades Union movement? I know you were involved in some pretty significant pieces of legislation...
I was very active in my union. I'm still proud of moving the first resolution on women's rights in 1975; and I wrote and taught what was I think the first feminist-criticism course in the UK, at Thames Polytechnic in 1977, where I'd been a lecturer since 1968. I was a member of the Communist Party, and wrote for Marxist journals like *Red Letters*. And of course I also later campaigned in the Women Oppose the Nuclear Threat group at the airbases in East Anglia and Greenham Common.
Your critical work bears the stamp of the politics; I'm thinking of that influential essay in Michelene Wandor's On Gender and Writing, *and your Virago books. It must have been hard, juggling all that:*

teaching, writing, political activism, travelling to and from London, family life.
As it always is for women. Little changes.

To go back to the poetry, your The East Anglia Sequence *enacts a very powerful searching of place. It seems a kind of precursor for your terrific sequence 'Alltud' which explicitly locates itself in Wales.*
I think that's true. Place has always been a big factor in what I've been writing; my response to the whole history, ecology, geography, whatever, of wherever I was. I would always want to do the sort of thing that I was doing in *The East Anglia Sequence*. It's true that I have to be really grounded in the area. Not passing through.
So that process of remaking you were describing doesn't alter your sense of cultural place?
Not basically. I had lived in East Anglia for over 20 years by the time of *The East Anglia Sequence* but fundamentally the Welsh connection held; its primacy was in the imaginary. For a while it was suspended, but only partially. When my mother died it flooded back.

You have remarked that, in a sense, you've always been struggling to get back to Wales. Does your mother have anything to do with that?
Yes. My mother was a strong influence on me and we had a close bond. It has sometimes seemed to me that everything I've been, creatively, is, in part, down to her. Not the academic side, but the poetic. She was probably one key source of the power, the attraction that remained for me in Wales, around the time my daughter Rhiannon was born in 1969.

You came to Wales from London as a small child. How did that happen?
The family – that is my mother and my older sister – were evacuated from London, to my grandmother's farm near Abergavenny in early 1944. My father had left us: after I was born my mother had a nervous breakdown and was hospitalised. I think Dad, who was in the army, tried to keep things together for about six

months and then we were sent to be looked after in the Norland Nursery, which was effectually functioning as a war-time refuge and orphanage for those who could afford to pay. I was about six months old and my sister was three and a half or four. My sister and mother went to Wales early in 1944, and I was sent to join them when the nursery building was destroyed by a doodlebug. I was still very little, so when I eventually arrived in Wales I didn't recognise my mother. My memory is of these great big people standing around in the hall at my grandmother's house, and I'm thinking, which is my mother? And that was why, in terms of constructed identities and constructed meanings of place and home and nation, Wales became so important to me. It was my first home.

Somewhere you talk about Wales as being a kind of subterranean force.
I think it's Protean for me; it keeps changing. It is partly Illyria, partly imaginary, but as I've said it was also the first place I knew. It was the place where I found the family, where I found space, and my mother. And we built a very close relationship.

I know you've been working on a book about your mother. Can you tell me a bit about her?
As a young woman she'd been a cellist. She was very creative. Before I was born she wrote for children, but she thought of herself as uneducated; she'd only had two years of schooling. Thanks to my stepfather, who was a very loving kind man, she remained creative but not in the way that she had been when she was a professional cellist. She continued to write, became a photographer and worked for the National Trust and magazines like *The Field*.

And although her family – your family – was embedded in Wales you've implied at times that it didn't seem comfortably part of its cultural context.
I think of it as the colonial thing. That's in my sequence 'The ABC of Writing' – and elsewhere. My aunts and my grandmother

were very English. That was I think one of the factors that made me a communist, from the Vietnam war onwards, until the early 80s when the Party imploded.

So your family circumstances helped to politicise you. Did you see it then?
I would name it later. What I would know, as a child, was that I felt instinctively comfortable outside, or in the kitchen, or wherever there were people at work. I trusted them. I would feel I could talk to them and get near to them, whereas I didn't seem to have any language in common with some of my own family. The other thing which was important in my childhood was that we were right on the edge of the valleys.

How did you experience the valleys?
In the early days I knew and felt the proximity of the coal mining. My first Welsh nurse in my grandmother's house, her husband was a miner. I remember her as a lovely warm person who would tell us stories. It was another connection to a real world as opposed to this slightly bizarre cold place I'd ended up in. But there was this other, different but very real world. And it was actually very close.

What about the rest of Wales?
To us, from the Marches, north and west Wales were like foreign countries. Apart from Pembrokeshire, where we went every year because my aunt had a cottage near Newport. It was called Cedar Cottage and it came over in packing cases after the war. We loved it. It sat in a field just above a very small cove, and when we first went there just after the war the ferry was still going backwards and forwards across the river so you could get to the beach and the big sands. My experience of the rest of Wales was that it was where we went picnicking, pony-riding, and camping as we got older. Up into the Black Mountains, and the Brecon Beacons. Swansea and Cardiff were my only experience of the 'bright lights'. I didn't go to London until I was fifteen. I went on some school trips to the Bristol Old Vic. There were lots of

reasons for going to Newport: shopping, swimming baths, and boyfriends, and the first espresso café… Cardiff was the big city with the theatre and pantomime; and we knew opera and rugby happened there though we never went. But of course my mother thought Cardiff was the centre of all sinfulness.

Were you always interested in poetry?
When I was somewhere between five and seven I started a novel about a swan but I got disheartened when I discovered I didn't know enough about swans. But I always loved poetry at school. Read it, learned it, though didn't write much before I started the Clare research, when I was about 23. I loved reciting poetry; I was always good at speaking and reading. I acted quite a lot, at school and at Cambridge, so that was all part of it. I would hunt through anthologies like *The Golden Treasury* for poems that were musical and lyrical. It was the movement and sound that bewitched me, rather than the rational content, what Pound calls melopoeia.

Do you remember any poets in particular?
Yeats when I was in my late teens. But also Robert Graves. Walter de la Mare, John Masefield, W.H. Davies. Herrick, Campion, other seventeenth century poets. And Hardy, the lyrics. And D.H. Lawrence.

I was wondering how much your childhood helped to inform the kind of worlds you seem to be sifting, or reaching past, in 'Alltud'?
Well it's another world. And it's not. Obviously things do change in time; but something remains. When I was writing 'Alltud' I think the haunting of my imagination by Wales had been sharpened by various factors to do with my marriage to Noel Bevan in the early nineties, and the times we spent in Wales together or separately. For example I went to Conwy on my own in 2007, searching after places my mother had been, following her maps, in her footsteps, as she photographed places for the National Trust. The last piece of the jigsaw of 'Alltud', the first to be actually written, was the Wye. We stayed in Erwood and explored all that area of Radnorshire.

I wrote the later sections in Aldeburgh, in the attic of my friend, the poet and Finnish translator, Bertie Lomas. The room was high up above the cold North Sea. In my mind was the map of Wales, particularly the whole central moorland and mountain-locked part. And I'm sitting as I write on the edge of the North Sea, which is as cold and grey and repellent as you can imagine, a hostile sea. So there are these contraries at work. But the deeper, buried movement is at the level of desire, in the analytic sense. At the deepest level of the psyche. So there are aspects of that poem which get carried along in the way that detritus is carried from a river's source to the sea.

Alltud means 'exile' in Welsh, of course. How did the title come about? Did you decide on it at the start?
No, it sort of emerged. I've thought a lot, since, about whether I should have called it 'exile' at all, and I'm not sure I should. I'm not sure that it's helpful. I think the danger of using a language which isn't yours, Welsh or French or whatever, is that it's as if you put it at several removes, in quotation marks. It's an allusion which you don't have to feel totally responsible for because it's somebody else's language. It gives hostage to people who query its use. I think I can understand where, as they say, that challenge is 'coming from'. But I don't think anybody should try to make exclusions about names you can and cannot use. It goes back to the multiplicity of voices. In some ways Wales is all the different sounds and voices of people living in Wales, English, Italian, Tamil, whatever. Like any country, it's a small polyglot place. What a word signifies to a native language-user has to be considered; of course I can't be aware of what the resonances of a Welsh word might be for a Welsh speaker. But anyway the more I think about the word 'exile' the less I feel that it's right for the poem. It's not really a geographical state I'm exploring. Or only in so far as it's metonymic of the larger, psychic, condition. Perhaps I should have left it untitled.

I wondered how – why – 'Alltud' came to be written at all?
The poem had to be written; as Alice Notley says, in one of her

titles, 'Alice ordered me to be made'. Well my unconscious ordered 'Alltud'.

So you don't necessarily 'come' to write a poem?
I think what I do is I realise that there is a poem that needs to be written. So now is the time consciously to make time available. In the old days I would go to Sennen (North Cornwall) with another writer friend. I don't do that any more, but it's a good thing to do. Go and sit there for three weeks and stare at the sea and live a disciplined, a kind of monastic, life. If you've got a piece that you know needs to be written, although you don't know what it is, that necessary straitening comes over you. Everything else seems less important.

I'm thinking that the sequence somehow expresses both the exploratory nature of your writing, in that it expands the singular lyric, but it also depends on a kind of straitening or self-disciplining.
I think that's right. I've always written sequences, although I have also made loose baggy monsters. It works for me to have a kind of coherent, discrete form that's flexible and can accommodate rapid changes.

Do you think that that very powerful sense of provisionality in the poetic and the imaginary is somehow charged by your analytical, Jungian work?
My Jungian reading and studies have influenced me quite deeply, but so does whatever's going on at the time of writing. Becoming a Catholic drew me more into ritual, wordless performance. A kind of indirection, a summoning, the old gods. At the level of the text I'm still going to work using repetition, collage, juxtaposition, cutting, the absurd, dream, different voices, layering – traditional 'modernist' techniques. That's my tradition, my late 20th century poetic inheritance if you like. The provisionality comes out of the uncertainty of what one's doing, of what one knows, if anything, of where it all leads. The older you get the more mysterious that is, so in the poem it's more and more like play or performance as in 'I CHINA AM'.

*Thinking back over your work, it seems as if it's those techniques –
that inheritance – which have largely held the ideological ideas at bay,
certainly in the last two or three decades.*
Ideology in poetry is for me a killer. My last years of political
engagement, mainly with the peace movement, were in the early
eighties. I was still involved in some ways; I sat on a housing
association executive, and I was a school governor, but I wasn't
involved in the trade union movement any longer. But gradually
the political commitments faded away. Sara [Maitland] and I did
the book on women saints – *Virtuous Magic* – and then eventually I went into Jungian analysis, and then into training.

Do you have an ideal reader?
Not any more! Though I have said, somebody with a very quick
intelligence, who hasn't got pre-formed ideas, who is open and
who is patient too. Who is prepared to stay with the knots and
difficulties of the surface of the text because they're there for a
reason. You do it that way because you need to; because that's the
only way you can express what has to be expressed. Ask any
painter. Ask any composer. People will accept it from painters
and composers. But they don't understand it in poetry. They
think the poem should enable you to understand your life better
or see things more clearly. They cannot seem to understand that
you have to learn to read each poet according to the needs of that
particular poet and/or poem.

*Perhaps we could talk about some of your more recent work? You
mentioned I CHINA AM, which appears – or part of it anyway – in*
The Land Between. *It's an interesting text, in a different mode
again...*
It's a vein of my work which comes about when I'm commissioned to do something for performance in public spaces. I've
done three major works in this vein in the last seven years. There
was 'The Unmaking', for a poetry festival in Cork in 2005, on
which I collaborated with the composer Michael Parsons. It's
about the nineteenth century clearances in the Hebrides; I spent
a lot of time in the archives on Skye and uncovered a mass of

material about the evictions of the crofters. Then, later in 2005, there was the performance piece, for voice and B flat drone, *I CHINA AM*, for 'Swayed To The West', an event organised by Nicholas Johnson and Etruscan Books to coincide with an exhibition staged by Bristol's Arnolfini Centre about the famous American liberal arts college in North Carolina, Black Mountain. The third piece, 'Cloud Cover Imponderable', was commissioned by the Parasol Foundation for the Contemporary Art gallery in Islington to accompany their 2009 Keith Tyson exhibition. Of the three only *I CHINA AM* is in print, and only partially, so they all remain as working texts, raided but not as yet entirely reproduced.

Are you still writing about Wales? Going to write about Wales?
I think what I've done lately to an extent – since Wales was (is) so bound up with (personal, unresolved) questions that bring into focus not just Noel but my whole life unreeling backwards – has been to set Wales temporarily to one side, so to speak; to turn my back on the family. With two close deaths in three years I haven't had the strength to continue looking the traumas of my early life in the face. Wales is irrevocably, inevitably bound up with those war-time traumas: of institutionalisation, separation and loss, late arrival. I needed, after 2008-2011, a fresh start. Another place. I found it in Orkney. These last two years I've been going up to Orkney as often as I can. My friend, the poet Nigel Wheale, lives and works there. In many ways it reminds me of the Wales of the 1940s-50s that I grew up in. The look of it, the people's friendliness, the reach that's still possible into a simpler past with its traditions, lore and rich speech. Poets can be absorbed into the island culture, witness George Mackay Brown: it's hospitable to artists and composers. I've made quite a few friends on the island. I can work there, and it feels like a second home – Wales, Orkney – in a way that East Anglia and Suffolk never have. So I try to get up there as often as I can.

The pull of the place again? Thinking about that, and going back to 'Alltud', that poem seems to me to work in an almost Jungian way,

from a quite contemporary moment back through and beyond labels,
beyond the regulating influence of language.

It's working towards being in the realm of the spiritual perhaps.
You have to go back through all the significant places of your life.
The things that have made me, that have made each one of us,
are not of course the same as those that have made, as it were, the
mystery of the lands of Wales. But they are analogous in the sense
that they are mysterious, and buried. And you have to go back
through it; you know that when you've been working in analysis.
You have to go back, and if you find a name for the experience,
well that's just a name: it provides release, temporarily, it makes
for reassurance, but it's still provisional. Next time you visit it can
have shifted. So 'Alltud' is as much about psyche and spirit as it
is about terrain or culture. I mean: 'I am gone from the places
that knew me...'

But the poem also seems to be about a process which comes very close
to mapping, somehow.

Well I love maps, and you're right about there being a sort of
feeling of mapping in *Alltud*. My map of Wales itself is falling
apart because it's so old. But maps don't always tell you what you
want to know. If you ask for a walking map of a district you don't
know, you can find you can't read it because there's nothing that
you recognise.

'Alltud' seems to confirm that Wales is more than a physical or
geographical place to you.

It is a real place; it is 'home', *heimat*, where I may always return.
The borderland Wales is my earliest childhood of memory, near
the Black Mountains. But Wales is also a country of the imaginary. So it's 'BOTH ... AND'. Exile isn't the right word for a
separated 'both/and' condition. It's not estrangement. It's like
being separated in life from people in your family, but you stay
connected and you reconnect the minute you meet up again. I've
always liked having it both ways.

Do you think you'll always end up writing about the separation?

Yes because of course it's to do with a deeper psychological reality; that's what interests me. Writers and poets in particular have to work a lot in the dark, like moles, at least in the early stages in the sense of an analytic role. Writing doesn't do the work of changing you, but it can do the work of getting you to recognise what's going on and that's the first step. I think that's what readers are doing for you a lot of the time.

So it's a mixture of self-knowing and not knowing. You wouldn't be the first poet to say that, of course
Yes. What you know is always what you don't know. The poem is writing out of what you don't know. That's surely the oldest lesson in the book: it's only in the process of the writing that you discover what and why you're writing...

Can you say what you discover?
I think you discover just the shape of ledge you're standing on at the moment. And a bit about the cliff face around you, and a bit about the weather. But it's only for that moment. It's going to be different of course, the next time you're on the ledge. There might be a bit of thrift, there might be a particularly good place for you to put your fingers in. Or there might be a nasty shock.

Given that provisionality, what does language offer us? Is language the ledge?
I suppose so. I mean, it's all we have to work with...

Thank you very much.

A shortened version of this interview, which has since been revised, originally appeared in *Poetry Wales* No. 46, issue 1, pp. 32-7.

SHEENAGH PUGH

Sheenagh Pugh is the author of fourteen full-length collections, including two selected works: *Crowded by Shadows* (Christopher Davies, 1978); *What a Place to Grow Flowers* (Triskele Books, 1979); *Earth Studies and Other Voyages* (Poetry Wales Press, 1982); *Beware Falling Tortoises* (Seren, 1987); *Selected Poems* (Seren, 1990); *Sing for the Taxman* (Seren, 1993); *Id's Hospit* (Seren, 1997); *Stonelight* (Seren, 1999); *The Beautiful Lie* (Seren, 2002); *What If This Road* (Gwasg Carreg Gwalch, 2003); *The Movement of Bodies* (Seren, 2005); *Long Haul Travellers* (Seren, 2008); *Later Selected Poems* (Seren, 2009) and *Short Days, Long Shadows* (Seren, 2014). In addition she has published two novels, a book of translations (*Prisoners of Transience*, Seren 1985), and a range of critical works including essays on translation and a critical monograph, *The Democratic Genre: Fan Fiction in a Literary Context* (Seren, 2005). She lived for many years in Cardiff, where she taught Creative Writing at the University of Glamorgan. She now lives in Shetland; this email was conducted by email.

Since email has made this interview possible, perhaps we could start with the web, which I know you use energetically? What does the internet mean to you as a writer?
I'm not massively techy. I can't use the microwave and only ever use one setting on the camera. The internet was different because I could see real advantages in it; I really like the way it removes geographical limits from friendship. And it was easy to learn html because it's just another language and I've always had a facility with languages. I embraced email with delight because I hate

using the phone; I like to have some distance and time to work out what I want to say. Sometime in the 90s I started using the blogging community *LiveJournal*, at first because it was the place where a lot of fan fiction writers hung out, and I'd got very interested in fan fiction; nobody had really written about it in a literary context and I was working on what became *The Democratic Genre*. I've still got a lot of online friends in that community so I stayed with *LJ* when I set up my writing blog. Facebook I'm on because so many writers and publishers use it. Twitter I don't use much myself, but I love following gifted tweeters. My favourite is John Prescott. Twitter is good for pointing people toward a blogpost or promoting gigs or books. I think writers are going to have to learn how to use all these means of getting to an audience in future.

You've written many dramatic monologues, and you've said how much you enjoy the freedom ventriloquising allows...
I did love being a vent act, partly for the freedom to get into another skin – I think I could have been a terrible ham actor, given the chance – but partly also for the freedom to be me without looking like me. I mean, if I wanted to write a very 'personal' poem I would make it about someone else, or at least write it in the third person and probably male – 'he' rather than 'I' – to give more distance. It's partly a dislike of confessional poetry, which tends to give me compassion fatigue. But I haven't written so many personal poems of late. I've written some in close-third, like the Murat Reis sequence, but fascinating as he was, I didn't want to be inside his skin; in many ways, the point was that no one, including him, was quite sure who or what he was.

You've written two novels. Does a different Sheenagh Pugh write your novels?
The second one, *Folk Music*, is all in first-person; there are about eight different voices in there and one chapter consists entirely of conversation between two of them. The chapter in Edo's voice took me the longest, because I started and abandoned it three times wondering how he would talk about a certain facet of his

nature, until it dawned on me that he didn't know about it. I did, he didn't. But you have to get seriously into someone's head before you figure that out. So I would guess it's the same me writing both forms.

Why write a novel rather than a poem? Why write a poem rather than a novel?
My default is poems; I'd rather write intense lyrical moments than the boring link bits you need in novels. I have written a novel when I saw no other way of handling the material. But it's a lot of work and for little more reward than poems in terms of fame and fortune.

I don't think I'm alone in being struck by the huge range of personae you've tried out over the years. Would you have a favourite?
My favourite persona, out and away, was Lady Franklin. She very nearly did become a novel, in fact, until I decided that the poem sequence was a good halfway house for the reasons I've just explained: I could develop character and theme but write only the lyrical and dramatic moments. While I was writing that sequence I felt she was inhabiting me and dictating; certainly my work rate, which is normally terrible, increased massively and I can only put that down to her; she used to read a book every day, whilst doing a hell of a lot else. She and her cousin went to a scientific lecture one afternoon and some silly fellow said, 'Why aren't you at home making a pudding?' She said, 'We did all that before we came out!' I wrote all those poems in a little over a month, which is unheard-of for me.

How did you find her? Was it through Franklin? Or perhaps she led you to him?
The Arctic led me to both; I have a fascination with northern latitudes. My original interest was in him and in the men who went in search of him, but the more I read, the more I realised that she had in effect reinvented him, created his legend. She was a writer, but she didn't work on paper – in fact when she was offered the chance to write an epitaph for his tomb, she couldn't,

which was a pity because Tennyson did it instead and made a right hames of it. In the dedication to her in that book, I said she never read novels but knew how to make heroes, and that was a fact; many men performed incredible feats of endurance and courage because they were inspired both by her and by the legend she had created around him.

Did anything else draw you to Franklin, other than the Arctic? You've talked about the urge to commemorate in writing, especially the overlooked or unheard. But men like Franklin and Parry weren't overlooked.

It was the Arctic, above all, that drew me to them. There's something specific, for me, about the whole idea of 'furthest north'; the South Pole holds no fascination for me. The epigraph of 'The Arctic Chart' sequence was Tennyson's remark 'there is nothing worth living for, but to have one's name inscribed on the Arctic chart', to have some feature in the then-largely uncharted Arctic named after oneself. There was a magnificent unreasonableness about the whole business of Arctic exploration and the men involved. It was no practical use, for a start; even if there had been a Northwest Passage, which there wasn't, it would have been little use for trade because you couldn't have predicted exactly where it would be navigable from one year to the next. As for the men who went there: Ross, who'd already spent 4 years marooned up there, couldn't get the Navy to accept him as a captain on their search for Franklin because he was over 70; so he fitted out a ship at his own expense, running into debt in the process, and went off searching, simply because he'd once given Franklin his word that he would. Elisha Kent Kane, another Arctic veteran, went on the search with a dicky heart which he, being a doctor, knew perfectly well would kill him before he saw middle age. René Bellot said that there was no sense of creed or country up there; the sense of universal brotherhood he felt caused him to start speculating about the possibility of an international organisation that would solve the problems that might otherwise cause wars. It's almost as if the extreme climate and geography called forth similar extremes in men. Parry was, of all of them, least like me; he was very religious and probably the hardest for me to empathise with because of that. I think I was trying to feel how the Arctic would have affected a man like him.

Were any of them like you? Would (could) you have been an explorer?
None of the Arctic explorers were like me; they were all physically brave, incredibly generous and had a terrific work rate. I don't identify with them. I have always preferred standing to one side watching other people do things. Nor do I want to produce art that is some sort of Mirror Of Real Life, much less of me; I prefer it to be a window on places I haven't been and things I haven't done.

Why is the 'furthest' North so fascinating?
I haven't a clue why, for me, the north compels more, unless it's the legacy of generations for whom, in the northern hemisphere, 'north' represents cold, extreme, highest on the map, whatever. I do know that Amundsen felt the same; one reason he got his work at the South Pole done so fast was that he had no desire to be there; he was itching to get back up north.

What is so special about Northern-ness?
It may well be partly the light, which has an extraordinary sharpness, and the air; where I live now, there are times when breathing is not so much automatic as a positive pleasure. I also like the extremes of light and weather, the odd things which being at such an acute angle does to light; I went to Trondheim in a snowy January once and the light was pink. The unimpeded sky, yes – I had a poem in *Poetry Scotland* about that called 'Big Sky', which ends

> It is as if,
> having lived all your life in the jewelled oval
> of a miniature, you stepped into a frame
> the size of a gallery wall, a landscape
> where a few small figures, lost against distance,
> seem to be looking for the way out.

I'm not sure that those lines don't sound like some kind of warning. You've used poems to reproach, as well as to elegize and commemorate, before now.

I wrote it because, having lived in cities most of my life, I was in a very different environment and found myself reacting to landscape differently in consequence. When I was an urban poet, I couldn't write about a landscape unless it had people in it. I was beginning to wonder why I had seen them as so important. Also I was getting older and feeling very conscious that said landscape was a lot more immortal than I was. My latest collection – *Short Days, Long Shadows* – is very mortality-haunted.

Did you write it in Shetland?

The collection was written partly in Cardiff and partly in Shetland, though there are also a few from travels in Norway.

Do you miss being in a city?

We get back to Cardiff every so often. And I've been to Edinburgh, Bristol and London on litbiz. So I'm not devoid of city streets should I want them. We had always intended to move to Shetland; we'd been spending time there for 20 years and my husband's asthma was far more controllable there than in Cardiff. But I can honestly say that I have never missed anywhere I once lived, however much I liked it at the time. I moved a lot as a child, and I think people with that experience protect themselves by being very easily uprooted. When I leave a place I put it in a box in my head called the past and stop thinking about it. Until recently, that was also true about the people who inhabited it – I've never been one for reunions, writing to old friends – but the internet has made things more global and friendships easier to keep up at a distance.

Why did you move around as a child? I know both sets of grandparents (one Irish, the other Welsh) ended up in the South Wales Valleys. I assumed that your family had moved there too.

My parents were teachers. They moved out of Wales originally because in the 50s and 60s Welsh authorities had a policy of not employing newly trained teachers; they told them to get a job in England and come back when they had more experience. Of course many never did come back; it was a selfish and short-sighted policy. They moved around in search of promotion; also it was easier to buy a house further north. I lived in Birmingham, though not long enough to recall it, then Essex, then Nottingham. I was very lucky to have gone to school there when the late John Neville was running the Nottingham Playhouse. I saw a lot of plays there and, I think, all the ones that were set texts for A-level; he made a point of trying to perform them for the kids. Makes a lot of difference.

What's it like where you are now?
More extreme; weather makes a lot more odds and there are far more noticeable seasonal differences. Just now in June it never gets properly dark at night, just vaguely blue; in December there'll be about four hours of real daylight and everyone rushing to get outdoor jobs done. Also a lot of stars and occasional auroras. All this has seeped through into my poems.

You've called nationality a habit. I'm wondering how living in Shetland might have altered how you think about Wales, where you forged so much of your writing career?
I was probably being flippant. I don't think about nationality much at all, and it isn't important to me. Shetland was Norwegian territory, then Danish, before it came to Scotland as part of some Danish queen's dowry. Obviously there is a lot of Scottish blood and tradition here now but also a lot of Norse, which meshes with my own fascination with all things Northern; I've always been mad on Icelandic sagas. I only really feel Welsh when English people are mispronouncing place names, or making stupid sheep jokes or just generally being English and superior without even realising it. My son still lives in Wales and I still have a Welsh publisher. It amuses me, occasionally, when some reviewer gets sniffy about my stuff not being particularly "Welsh": I publish with a Welsh house and always have, which is more than that great "nationalist" R.S. Thomas did. I don't, so

far, think more about Wales than I used to but I haven't been away from it very long. At the moment I'm very into living next to the sea, which I've never done before and was long my ambition. I absolutely love waking in the morning and seeing the ocean out of my window, and the sea's coming into my poems even more than ever, and in a different way.

You've only really talked about Shetland in terms of its landscape?
Are there people nearby? Do you avoid neighbours?
There are plenty of people: we live in a small village where for the first time that I can recall, I know the names of my neighbours. Actually that makes it harder to write about them, though I have, suitably disguised.

Do you enjoy living in such a small community? Do you feel at home?
I enjoy living in the village, yes. It's small enough to feel like a community and contains a lot of interesting people. As for feeling at home, like I say moving about a lot as a child has left me disinclined to see anywhere as permanent. Shetland folk, and Scots as a whole, don't say 'I live in X'; they say 'I stay in X', which sounds ominously temporary, as if they're always conscious of being transient creatures, which of course we all are.

To go back to your poems, the voices don't only liberate you bodily and
psychologically. You've said you often find your subjects in history
books. Can you say anything about the allure of the past? Why time-
travel?
Confucius says, 'Men's natures are alike; it is their habits that drive them far apart'. As long as I can remember, I have been drawn to poems that play on this likeness of nature, when you read and think 'I've been there', which crashes all barriers of age, sex, nation or time. It is one reason I've always loved translation. When Ibykos, at 90, falls in love again and compares himself to a tired old racehorse forced to drag itself round the track one more time; when the anonymous mediaeval Irish monk somewhere in Austria tells us how much he loves his one companion, his tauto-logically-named cat Pangur Ban; when Walt Whitman writes of

dreaming he was naked in the street, they come very close to us; you sense their essential humanity and likeness to yourself. Also, of course, the best stories are all in history books. I don't quite go with Beryl Bainbridge's 'what's the point of making anything up when there's so much history?' because to me history is material, and ripe for embroidery like any other subject matter. But if you made up some of the true stories in history books, critics would call them far-fetched. I'm toying just now with the story of a Roman tombstone from Africa; apparently it reads 'Here Lies [Insert Name Here]'. That tells historians that masons and their apprentices couldn't necessarily read; they worked from templates, and in that case you can imagine the master's left the job to the lad, who can't read and has laboriously copied what he sees on the template. And then the master's gone along with it, presumably because the client couldn't read either. I find that intensely moving, like the tokens which some transported convicts left for their families, and for which they often had to rely on people who could read and write. The thought of being deprived of that, of having to trust someone else to convey your meaning because you hadn't words, is one that really gets to me.

I tend to think of poets as being part of some kind of place or community, but also standing apart. Do you think of yourself as having a public role?
My poems are surely far more conscious of landscape than when I lived in a city, but I think themes and concerns probably change more with age and approaching death than anything else. I have written poems that comment on public events, but "having a public role" sounds quite alarming. I admire what some poets have tried to do with that, notably the way Andrew Motion, when Laureate, set up the Poetry Archive, but I'm quite glad that I'm never likely to be in such a position. I am not sure poets have to be "for" anything, except maybe entertaining the reader. I am suspicious of agendas. By nature, I am not one of the world's joiners-in. Georges Brassens' song '*La mauvaise réputation*' pretty much nails it for me: '*Le jour du quatorze juillet | Je reste dans mon lit douillet. | La procession qui marche à bas | Cela ne me regarde pas.*'

'When the procession passes by / I lie in bed and close my eyes.
/ If they want to have their jubilee, / That's got nothing to do with
me.' (My translation, by the way, and not literal.) Even in my
dreams I have always been a voyeur, standing by looking at things
happening to other people rather than having them happen to
me. That's quite useful for a writer, and it may be part of the
reason I became one, but I would still be that way if I'd never
written a word. I write because I enjoy it, because I can, because
it enables me to get across things I want to express and communicate, but above all because it offers some slim chance of living
on, even if only for a little while, after I'm dead. This is quite a
powerful incentive for an atheist. It's also behind the impulse to
commemorate other people.

Were you always atheist?
My parents weren't religious. My father, in his early twenties, was
in the navy during World War II and was deeply shocked when a
bishop blessed their battleship before they went off to kill people.
He didn't doubt the need of killing people, at the time; he just
thought bishops shouldn't be complicit in it and I don't think he
ever troubled a church again. I think it's ludicrous to assume an
omnipotent being would allow suffering, or that if it did, it would
be worth worshipping. There's a story about Randolph
Churchill, who wasn't all that bright, to the effect that one of his
friends bet him he couldn't read the whole Bible. He went off to
do so, came back in a week and said 'That God – what a bastard!'
Not that stupid, then.

*You have written critically, both on translation and on 'fanfic'. But
you don't like critics much, do you?*
Some critics are very good at what they do, but some, and I don't
mean just the broadsheet guys, are downright lazy or ill-
informed. A few are mendacious, deliberately misrepresenting
books by either choosing quotes very selectively or actually
writing lies. I don't read Lit Crit. It's the single most uncongenial
genre, to me. I wrote it because I got paid to. I only write reviews
to bring writers who might otherwise be neglected to more notice.

Why did you write about fanfic?

Because I was very interested in it, and nobody else, at that time, was considering it as a literary genre. The thing about fan fiction is, it dissolves boundaries. I love anything that blurs boundaries. First, no fanficcer has any artificial respect for the author's primacy; they're quite happy to say the original author doesn't know everything about his/her characters. I've long thought that when Austen makes Darcy say 'dearest, loveliest Elizabeth' she is just plain wrong: the man would never utter those words. But the other more exciting boundary it blurs is between reality and fiction. If a fictional character has measurable effects in the world, if people do, write, think things they wouldn't have otherwise because of him, if they feel emotions like love for him and grieve when he 'dies', then in what sense is he not 'real'? I'd suggest, only in the quite narrow one that he can't in his own person walk down a street. (TV and film characters of course can do even that via their actor, and plenty of those come to identify with their characters to the point of channelling them). My sequence 'Fanfic' was about that blurring, and so was 'Lady Franklin's Man' (*The Beautiful Lie*). He is her man in the sense of husband but also her creation; in a very real sense she creates a fanfic version of him. Murat Reis goes further; he makes a fictional version of himself which takes over from the real one to the extent that others begin ficcing this persona, as 'Matthew Rice' (though I was also, of course, poking fun there at the English inability to recognise that there are other languages in the world. It was true, though; people did claim to recall the imaginary Matthew.)

You've said you often find your personae, especially the historical ones, by reading. Do you like the research?

Doing the research is fun, because I never set out to do it. I just read what interests me and then write about it. I read history books like novels. Obviously it's different researching for novels, because it's a more detailed world and you start worrying about whether you've got it 'right' – not that a novel should have to be true to history in all respects, but if it isn't, somebody will undoubtedly carp about it.

Can we take the boundary-blurring back to poetry, and genre in particular? Form offers poets boundaries. How do you decide what form might suit a poem?

The question of form interests me. I tend to go mad on a particular form for a while and then have to force myself out of it. For a long time it was what I call Doty couplets, i.e. unrhymed 2-line (or sometimes 3-line) verses *à la* Mark Doty. Then I began to feel there wasn't enough music going on and wanted a stricter form. Loose *terza rima* often works well for me, and I also lately fulfilled a lifetime ambition when I finally found a subject that suited the sestina – I got a sequence of three, called 'Walsingham's Men', published in *PN Review*. The default for me at the moment is a form of sonnet with an odd rhyme-scheme that crosses the couplet, so that it goes ab-bc-cd-de-ef-fg-ga. The idea is to set up a tension between couplets of sense and couplets of rhyme. When I say rhyme, of course they're mostly half-rhyme or near-rhyme: I can't generally be doing with full rhyme because I want the sound pattern to be more subtle than that. I've written shedloads of those sonnets; the Webcam Sonnets, several of the 'Murat Reis' poems, lots of others in *Long Haul Travellers*, and there are more in the last collection – along with the Walsingham sestinas and a fair few in *terza rima*. I would never have figured out how I could do the Walsingham poems without seeing Paul Henry's disguised sestinas in 'The Brittle Sea', which he masks by putting the line and verse breaks in unexpected places, not on the rhyme-words. I think it was also Henry's work that made me feel that free verse wasn't giving me enough music. I would write more free verse if I could do it like Louise Glück, whose language has incredible stillness and intensity. But not all the poets you like actually influence your own writing. I can't do Glück, alas.

'The Boyhood of Tristran Jones' uses a split line in ways which seem to me to point up the whole boundaries thing, and not just in theme. I noticed it in 'Murat Reis' too. I like the way it admits both spaciousness and control. Did you find it somewhere?

I think the split line came from the poetry of Rosie Shepperd, whose work I like a lot. She's very adventurous with the line, uses white space to great effect. I've always rather liked strong caesuras, especially when they happen in unexpected places, and you could argue that the split in the line is just a caesura, maybe.

Yes. Because they're half or fragments of single lines, they lengthen whichever line you want to join them up with, preceding or following. But you can as easily read them as foreshortened whole lines.
I honestly don't know if that's in my mind when I'm writing. I just sound it in my head and try different ways until it feels right. I've written a sonnet and then recast it as free verse, before now, when it became clear that those clothes didn't suit it. This is making me feel as if I ought to have some logical way of justifying how I work, but I really just make it up as I go along! I see something new and think 'I'll have a go at that' and it might work or it might not.

Thinking about space – it's a word which often appears in your work. Not necessarily the out-there space; it's just as often to do with room/opportunity, and/or absence…
I see white space as part of the pattern, like the lead in the stained glass. I also think this applies to some extent in life; the white spaces are as real as the inhabited ones. The nineteenth-century Dorset dialect poet William Barnes is incredibly good at creating the space where a person used to be, but now is not. He does it literally in 'The Turnen Stile', where a family who have lost a child go through a turnstile and at the end of the poem, the father automatically turns back, looking for the child, but sees only the empty arms of the stile standing still, where once they would have spun with the boy between them. He does the same thing in other bereavement poems like 'Woak Hill', 'Tokens' and 'The Wife a-Lost' amongst others. I think one reason this skill of his fascinates me so much is my interest in history and archaeology, which gets stronger the more I myself resemble an old fossil. I can't look at an old building, or a patch of ground, without getting a sense of all the things that may have happened there, all the people who have walked that ground, and who aren't there now, who have left spaces where they once were. There's a poem in *Long Haul*

Travellers called 'Regina' which is my attempt at a Barnesian creation of space where a person used to be, the 'ungoverned house' bereft of the wife, which now feels colder to the husband than the outside world does.

It's been a long career. What have been the highlights, for you?
Well, winning the Forward individual poem prize, Cardiff International Poetry Prize and Bridport Prize (twice, I think), plus getting shortlisted for the Whitbread was quite nice, though it makes less difference than you'd think in terms of publicity and sales.

You're very down-to-earth about your writing, but you've also talked about wanting to leave a mark behind you.
I want to leave something because I don't believe in life after death in the religious sense, so the only way not to be totally extinguished is to leave something that will outlive you. Ideally it'd be a poem – not the dreaded 'Sometimes', obviously – still getting anthologised and being a part of the canon, whatever that is. Maybe the website will outlive me.

Thank you very much.

DERYN REES-JONES

Deryn Rees-Jones has published five collections of poetry: *The Memory Tray* (Seren, 1994); *Signs Round a Dead Body* (Seren, 1998); *Quiver* (Seren, 2004); *Falls and Finds* (Shoestring Press, 2008); *Burying the Wren* (Seren, 2012). *And You, Helen*, a poem and long autobiographical essay on the widow of Edward Thomas, was published by Seren in 2014. Editor of *Modern Women Poets* (Bloodaxe, 2005), and co-editor (with Alison Mark) of *Contemporary Women's Poetry: Reading/Writing/Practice* (Palgrave Macmillan), she has produced a number of critical works, including *Carol Ann Duffy: Writers on their Work* (Northcote House, 1999) and *Consorting with Angels: Essays on Modern Women Poets* (Bloodaxe, 2005) and a critical edition of Marie Stopes' novel, *Love's Creation*. With Ralph Pite, she edits the scholarly 'Poetry &' series and is the editor of the new poetry imprint, Pavilion, at Liverpool University Press. She lives in Liverpool, where she is Professor of Poetry at the University of Liverpool.

You were made Professor of Poetry in 2012. You've said you never intended to be an academic, but you've achieved so much as both poet and critic; is it a relief to be recognised for that?
I didn't want to be an academic particularly; I wanted to carry on thinking about poetry. I wanted to write a thesis. I wanted to explore what I wanted to explore in a context that I felt would be provoking and sustaining. Twenty years on I am glad to be recognised for what I am doing. That's not just because it's been a lot of hard work, and it has been, but also because it confers value

on the work – writing about poetry by women. I really like teaching, and I like being in a university because I feel it still is – just about – a place where you can be free to have and exchange ideas. I value the rootedness of a job, because it brings freedom. But it is also demanding. I juggle my academic and poetic lives – sometimes I feel like I am juggling torches of fire – and in the past I've always probably given more priority to the demands of the academic life. Now maybe I can actually give priority, personal priority, to the poetry.

The title is nicely open-ended, isn't it? You can be a poet who also writes about poetry.
Yes. I always want to be able to do both, the critical and the creative work. I didn't teach Creative Writing here at Liverpool for a long time. I taught Creative Writing a little at Liverpool Hope. We started an MA in Writing, but not long after that I left for my current job. I think I decided when I left that I wasn't going to do creative writing any more. I'm not sure why. There was something purist about it, but also probably protective, keeping my poetic self away from my professional self. I wanted to embed myself in literature and the reading of it.

Is there a sense in which the criticism feeds the poetry?
Criticism makes me think in a way I wouldn't in any other area of my life. But it's not an easy thing for me.

So why carry on?
Because it's good for me! It's the moralist in me: this is hard, this is difficult; and there is a pleasure in the challenge of that, shaping thoughts, making arguments. I don't think I ever want an easy life in that respect, of being free to duck away from a necessary and sustained working with and through complex and difficult and always energising ideas. For some people I suspect that is an easier choice. Or maybe that's my fantasy! Certainly writing criticism in the way I would like to doesn't come as easily to me as writing poetry. It's a balance and a tension, and I think my poems grow a lot, quietly, because of what I'm reading and

writing about. I have to read, and think, in that way…

And the Chair helps to authorise that balancing act? Gives it space?
I think of it as recognition that my critical writing and my poetry
go hand in hand. And I'm using it as a chance to think about
creative writing and creativity more specifically. I wanted to
probe that for myself. I've always been interested in the relationship between the arts and sciences, and it's an opportunity to
think more generally about what we do when we imagine. We're
building a PhD programme that has real world contexts (work in
mental health, and with architecture for example) and inter-
disciplinarity as its underpinning. The role (these days it is a role)
gives you the chance to see if you can make an idea happen. So
it brings authority and confidence, which helps in all sorts of
ways. But I don't write as a 'Professor of Poetry'. I never will.
Who would! I still feel a considerable responsibility to write about
poetry by women, to understand what's going on. As one of the
people who also write about women's work you'll know the
feeling of there never having been many people who do. But at
the same time – and this is really starting to happen now – you
see new young critics coming up who are writing about, really
opening up debates in, contemporary poetry and rooting their
engagement in work by women. And that's quite a relief: in terms
of having a community of critics to exchange ideas with, and to
bounce ideas off, for one thing; but also feeling (it's not quite like
this, but it is a part of it) you don't have to take responsibility for
doing it all the time yourself. The work is being done… So for the
first time now I'm also writing about male poets.

What are you working on at the moment?
I'm writing about Edward Thomas; about language and music
and Welshness. I'm thinking about him and Helen Thomas – their
marriage – as a way of thinking about gender, and muses, and
marriage and parenting and widowhood… and poetry. I'm
writing a poem – from the point of view of Helen Thomas – at
the same time as a critical essay. A proper synergy: as I write
some things go in the poem and are pulled out of the essay, and

vice versa. Which in itself feels a bit of a risk. I'm fascinated by
Helen. And I'm questioning along the way exactly why I'm so
drawn to her.

So it's Helen rather than Edward? Or both?
She and Edward Thomas work as a sort of split for me so you get
Thomas the poet, Thomas the difficult character, Thomas
negotiating his Welshness and having that complicated relationship with Wales which I think I share; and Helen Thomas is this
remarkable person who suffers and mothers and…

Endures? That's my impression of her.
Absolutely. I'm very interested in that idea of endurance. I picked
on them as a couple because they're speaking in a way about me
and things I'm resolving or recognising, well, as a single parent
really. That idea of how you mother and how you poet? At the
same time. So they've become a bit of a trope for me to work that
off… You don't come away from their story thinking 'poor Helen
Thomas'. She has too much agency, too much strength for that,
despite having such a difficult life.

*You make them sound conjoined. And as if you find yourself in both
of them.*
You do step back and think why am I doing this? Why am I
obsessed with this? And there's always a reason, isn't there, for
whatever you write about?

Do you think you're drawn to Helen because you'd have liked her?
I don't know if I'd have liked her. I have huge admiration for her.
She writes very well. And she was passionate and managed,
either by temperament or sheer force of will, or a combination of
the two, to be incredibly resilient and to nurture those she loved.
She loved Edward, the way he saw the world, and the way he
showed her a different way of seeing the world. I'm not for a
moment tempted to be an advocate for romantic love that in fact
is a false narrative, that legislates suffering, or bad behaviour in
its name. But I do think that the bonds – sexual bonds, romantic

bonds, familial bonds, as well as bonds of friendship that are also about love – are complex and remarkable; and sometimes we take them for granted. As a culture we fetishize them and divert them into very reduced single narratives of sex or desire. And while poetry has historically done its fair bit of that, it manages the complexity better, and the joys and pains and ambiguities better, and is a natural place through which to explore them.

Have you ever tried to bring creative and critical modes together so deliberately before?
No, I haven't. I'm really excited because I'm working with a wonderful London-based artist, Charlotte Hodes, and along with her pictures we're going to make an animation. We were introduced through a close mutual friend, the poet and translator Tony Rudolf. In the poem I wanted to talk about the idea of Edward going off to the war. I've thought a lot about women writing narratives in time of war, like H.D. and the Irish poet Sheila Wingfield. I've never written about them but they're very alive in my consciousness, those big poems that deal with war from the female point of view. And I wanted to do that with the 1914 centenary in mind.

Didn't H.D. and Imagism help nudge you into writing in the first place? Do you look at figures like that differently now?
You do look at them differently, but I think as a poet you come back. Once something is read it can never be forgotten. You start off with this map and it unfurls. You keep wandering round, rediscovering that first map your writing created. I don't want to keep on writing the same poem, but that's sort of what you do do, and it's finding a different way to do that that's so important. I'm quite conventional about the words on the page, the left hand margin, all that. I want to shake myself up a bit. You have to push yourself...

Do it the hard way?
[*Laughs*] At the end of the day if I write a poem that has a kind of music to it, that gives me pleasure, I'm happy. But working out

how to do it – because every time you do it you forget – yes, that's hard...

You mentioned Wales in connection with Thomas. You were nominated for the 2013 Wales Book of the Year Award for Burying The Wren. *I know you've not always felt accepted as a Wales-identifying writer, but you've also described the hospitality you've experienced in Wales...*

I am very glad to be thought of as a Welsh writer. But I also feel because of my own experiences that national identification – like gender identification – is always more complicated than it might at first seem. I've spoken elsewhere about that idea of having a Welsh imagination, of Wales for me being a place to write *from*. My paternal grandmother grew up on a Welsh farm. From the mid seventies most of my summers were spent in North Wales while my father remained in Liverpool working. So I think the place from which I write is very much influenced by my time in rural Wales, but in the company of the English side of my family, and operating under maternal law! If it left me feeling slightly disconnected at the same time I always felt I was connecting with a familial and important part of myself, my backstory, if you like, as I was there. I still spend quite a bit of the week in Wales. I drive back and forth; to cross over the border is only forty minutes – and I'm in the landscape and hearing spoken Welsh, and that's very important to me.

You've also said you feel Liverpudlian. I think I think of you as having a foot on both sides.

If you say 'I'm a Liverpool writer', people can misunderstand that. It becomes a cliché. Not everyone would hear the subtext of Wales and Ireland in that history, in being 'from' Liverpool in terms of all its hybridities.

It seems to be about belonging. Even as a child weren't you wanting to make connections? I'm thinking of the Welsh phrase book you bought for yourself...

Some of it comes down to being named. I cannot escape my name: it's how people relate to me, my primary identifier! I gave my daughter a Welsh name, but she's also got a different kind of hybridity to negotiate. My husband had his own complicated relationship with his Irishness, and that was a strong bond between us. He was adopted, but he grew up in Liverpool and then found his Irish family and was very adamant that he wanted his children to have Irish passports. So they travel on Irish passports and when they're with their Irish cousins they suddenly get Irish voices... and the Irish get Scoused! So in some ways it has become very important in our family to identify via the simultaneous complications of connection and estrangement and all the politics of that.

Isn't it exciting to have this to reach into, a kind of cultural album? Does part of you enjoy the complexity?
I'm aware it is working strongly in *Burying the Wren,* and in fact, in more recent bird poems that connect me with my name. What happens is that the poems do the work for you and then you start reading them back and you get glimpses of understanding. Poems are always full of premonitions. I mean, there you are, a little knotted self and the poem sends out these threads and shoots, and you follow them along, trust the thread and then you get somewhere and then 'Oh, I see...' [laughs] *'that's* my preoccupation!' Actually it varies: there's a lot about life and death, and about birds – moving from the underworld, choosing between life and death – in my work. Probably that border of betweenness at some level is the Welsh-English border too; it's in my emotional blueprint now. It's written in. But the difficulty – sometimes it can feel like a difficulty – around national identity also gets overlaid. And the life and death thing has always been in my work, along with desire, too, so I feel when I am writing now that the work is thickening and deepening, but also that I am continuing to throw out the shoots, gather threads.

Are you superstitious? I've been conscious of a strong sense of other-worldliness in your writing. I wasn't sure whether you were religious. If you're not, it begins to seem...
I'm a great rationalist and I'm a great pragmatist. But I definitely

do all that magical thinking stuff, and I keep it well at bay too.

The pragmatism is a defence?
It's a way of operating and being; that's fine. But I also think, you know, I'm a poet. If I can't think magically who on earth can? The first essay that I wrote on Edward Thomas is about poetry and magic. It's on his poem 'Rain'. Rain and weather have always been important to me in the poems as well, that fluctuating trans-forming moodiness.

Why?
It's weather's openness to an internal and an external state at the same time. I probe that, and how you make something in a poem happen. I'm not going to make it rain by writing a poem about the rain, but at some level do I ever think I might? So I am interested in what I think I might do by writing those words on the page, and I don't know whether I believe it or not. Magic is about trust, somewhere, isn't it? As well as fear. It's about belief and letting go of things; keeping your feet off the ground... having a certain kind of control, that childish feeling of a kind of omnipotence.

Isn't it also about a kind of naivety? Doesn't magic allow us to imagine things which aren't possible?
Magic allows you to make connections. Of course if you make too many connections you're paranoid. But I have to do a lot of very rational competent dealing-with-stuff. Parenting, working, those things are all about responsibility, and thinking about other people, and conducting myself sometimes in a very public way. I take those responsibilities very seriously. Poetry is increasingly becom-ing the place for me to find freedoms, effectively to misbehave.

I think I'd have said that the earlier books are interested in misbehav-iour, but perhaps not formally? In some ways Quiver *seems more self-confident, more courageous.*
Thank you. *Quiver* was very painful to write. It was a big journey for me: I wrote it just after my second child was born. I felt it was addressing difficult things that people really didn't want to think

about and I felt a bit vulnerable. I was writing about things that were totally central to me; about what it means to be creative, to be a mother. And it felt, at the time, like those things weren't valued. But that's why you go on and write the next book.

In a sense, formally, Burying the Wren *seems more relaxed, for all the rawness.*
In fact *Burying the Wren* didn't happen as a direct consequence of my husband's death, although it is a book of elegies. A great deal of it was written before Michael died; it was beginning to come together ten years ago, when I was doing *Quiver*. The book is about having children, about a hard time, a hard place. When you become a parent you're growing and changing a lot, too; you're learning a lot about yourself when you don't quite appreciate even that that is the case, because the focus is on your children, and that whole bodily negotiation with the world through pregnancy and breastfeeding and physically caring for this tiny human being. And absolutely simultaneously you've got to negotiate the way your partner deals with these changes, with these little others as selves, and their needs, all the time, and you're wondering where you are and losing yourself a bit in the process.

Yes I read them both very much as a parent, and – especially in respect of Burying the Wren – *in terms of that struggle. Are you saying* Quiver *took more out of you?*
When I finished *Quiver* I felt that was it. I really couldn't write anything for what seemed ages. And I've never had that feeling before. It was hell. Absolute hell. I was just trying to screw poems out. Hating them. I had to change my whole writing practice. I was used to writing poems very quickly, often with a piece of critical writing on the go at the same time. Poems are always hard work, but for me the hard work could happen intensively and at speed. Part of that is about having time to immerse yourself in the writing. I used to work with bits of scrap paper; I didn't care about things being lost because there was always something else [*laughing*]. I was that cavalier! But as the demands on my time became fiercer, every little thing I wrote had to go in a notebook

or it would have been lost. I have had to learn to write more slowly, from the heart of my family life rather than in writerly isolation from it.

Did it help that you could turn to writing critically?
Definitely. I'm really interested in the differences between the kinds of writing. Like a lot of poets, it's a way of being, thinking, for me. It's how I operate, it's how I function. Just the doing of it keeps me going.

You've talked about the danger of constructing writing as therapy; you don't mean that do you?
I don't think writing is therapy. I think it can be therapeutic and that's very different. The kind of dialogue you get in the psycho-analytic process is very similar to what happens when you are writing poetry. But when you're writing you're writing on your own; in an analytic context you're doing that in a living dialogue, based on provisionality. It's not the dialogue of you and the page. The psychoanalytic process oils the wheels; it can also stop you in your tracks. And it can stop you from getting too stuck, enmired with a habitual, or habituated and perhaps unhelpful version of the self.

You've argued that poetry is always about loss; I take that to mean that any poem can be read as a space in which language is used to negotiate some kind of desire, and thus mitigate some kind of loss. So perhaps any poem is invested with some sense of its own healing properties?
Certain poems seem to make people want to tell you things. People want the dialogue. They want to give you their story in exchange for the experience of the poem. That happens a lot. I've talked with other poets about what you do with that other story people sometimes need you to hear. Because poetry makes space for people to feel, connect and make connections, and I think you have a responsibility as a poet to hold that, somehow. It is a social function of poetry: why on earth in this technological age do we still do this thing called a poetry reading? Because it is an impor-

tant social act: people are in a room, sometimes sitting in darkness as they look at you, listening and feeling and thinking silently together and being guided through something by a poem's voice. I don't think you have to somehow take on another's burden completely, individually, or even collectively, but I think a poet has a role in assembling something in a public process; and that role has ancient roots, and we should value it.

Can we go back to the dialogue between you and the poem? I was thinking about your dramatic monologues, and about Elisabeth So. Who is or was she?
I was going to start writing full time as Elisabeth So. To send out poems and publish as her. I wasn't going to be me any more. I was thinking 'I'm sick of being me. I'm just going to be somebody else and see what happens when I send her work into the world.' I'm not sure that poem is dramatic in the sense of it being a dramatic monologue; she and I are closer than that. Elisabeth is my middle name, and is also my maternal grandmother's name. It is now also my daughter's middle name. My grandmother played a huge role in bringing me up, and I had a deep connection with her. So – I say this at readings – the name Elisabeth So signals, 'So what?' But it's also sewing, about binding something up, I think.

It sounds Asian...
In my mind she was partly Chinese. At the start I wrote a little paragraph about where she was and what she'd done, and I started reading lots of Chinese literature in translation. My maternal grandmother had a relationship with a Chinese guy in the thirties and I remember seeing these books that he'd inscribed to her and I was just so interested in what would have happened to her if she'd married him. My grandmother was part Irish, part Scottish on one side; a Liverpool mixture again.

And there is a Chinese, or part-Chinese figure in Quiver.
Elisabeth So was probably as a direct result of *Quiver*. I say I wasn't writing, but in fact that sequence came very quickly. It took me by surprise. I was reading a lot of Coetzee. He invents

that other, an alter ego named Elizabeth Costello. I'm really influenced by him I think.

You say you're close, you and Elizabeth So; is she an alter ego, or is that too reductive?
When you write an 'I', or write from that place in a poem, it is and it isn't you; it's a very special place. When I read that poem, I'm not Elisabeth So but I'm not me either. You become a voice. That's what's so interesting. You climb into language somehow, and I love that, actually. One of the things I love about reading is that I am in my poem. So when I read the dog poems, for example, which are much more difficult for me to read in a way, I am trusting language, trusting whatever self it is I'm finding in those words, but also finding how it connects to a bodily me.

Do you think that trust is well-placed? I think of language as being so treacherous, I'm not sure (as a reader) that I dare place that kind of trust in the language of any text.
Well yes. And I'd have agreed with that before my husband fell ill. But it's all we have, isn't it? When Michael was ill he lost language. Because of where the tumour was in his brain, his speech came and went. He lost his ability to read a linear narrative, but he could read poetry until really quite late on. I could read him certain novels that he could understand because they were more metaphorical or there was something about the language and the way the syntax worked. Ordinary linear syntax he couldn't do. When you see somebody opening their mouth and not making that connection, experiencing that aphasia, where you have something in your mind and you cannot put a sound to it... there is something terrible about that. What do you do when you don't have words? It made me reassess my own relationship to language, especially the way words can be defensive and stand not just for but in the way of feeling. That's all poets try to do, really: to open things up, to allow something to be meaningful in language. It taught me a lot about not needing to talk everything through. I'm learning to negotiate silence much better as I get older. I'm with Wittgenstein here; about some

things being unsayable. You can also learn not to say things and see how that *feels*.

Which poets do you turn to?
I'm reading lots of Edward Thomas, of course. And right now I think many of us are re-remembering what Heaney did. 'The music of what happens' has been a really resonant little touch-stone for me, as for many. *Field Work* is still a central book for me. I had 'The Glanmore Sonnets' very much in mind when I was writing the Elisabeth So sequence. Likewise as I was finishing *Burying the Wren* I was writing lectures on Dylan Thomas and Ted Hughes. Just the practical negotiation of writing a lecture and writing poems at the same time became crucial to my think-ing about language and meaning and music. And that's when you realise just how much what you read changes what you write. I love Auden, too. And Donne and Larkin would be in that list of touchstones as well.

What about women? I was wondering whether people like Denise Riley, Veronica Forrest-Thompson were partly behind your re-think-ing of your approach to the page and the margins and so on?
You couldn't get two poets more unlike than Denise Riley and Seamus Heaney but I definitely want them both. I love Riley, and Forrest-Thompson. I like the way they use irony, much as I like it in Larkin or Virginia Woolf. We started an MA module on Women Poets and Philosophy – I think teaching that's really helped me. Jorie Graham I really love. Anne Carson. I've learnt so much from other women writing, in different ways and at different stages. Jo Shapcott, for example; she's doing something so clever and so groundbreaking in terms of gender. I've written about Alice Oswald. I'm always interested in what she's doing because she comes from a very unexpected place; and Lavinia Greenlaw. I feel as a woman who is writing very lucky to have peers and predecessors who are opening things up, showing that there are different ways of writing as a woman that are not neces-sarily about gender, but do perhaps come from a negotiation with gender. And I will always read Gwyneth Lewis's work. I will

always have a very lively sense of what she's doing and it will always be important for me.

How did you get to know her?
We met in Hay on Wye; we did a week's workshop with Les Murray and became good friends. It is a really, really important friendship. Has been and always will be I think.

Do you talk about Wales? About Welshness?
We did at the beginning. All the time. She talked a lot about that negotiation with the international. It's important because she writes in the language of my silent self, the language I don't know. She moves across and between in a way I can't. I'm still not sure why I haven't learned Welsh, because I should, although I started to learn a little bit in the 1990s. The more I reflect on this, the more I become aware that when I began writing seriously in Bangor in the 1980s, not speaking Welsh became foregrounded; it brought together all sorts of other things, and was a strong unspoken part of the impetus to write. It was a tension, another loss to negotiate. I wonder if I learned Welsh now whether my 'poetic problem' would effectively be solved. No more need for poems. And I'm aware of all the complications of thinking or even saying that. And also that 'the poetic problem' can and must change for you as a poet. Maybe that's happening for me now. A friend recently suggested I do some Welsh/English translations/versions, and in fact that's my current project.

No more need ... I think that need has come very strongly through in this conversation. Can you ever imagine not feeling it?
Is writing everything to me? No, it absolutely isn't. Without it I would be very disoriented though. It is part of the way I exist and make meanings for myself. If I had suddenly to stop I'm sure I'd find other things to do. Maybe those things would be better for me. But the best answer I can give to the question is a simple, cheerful one. Can I ever imagine not feeling a need to write? No.

Thank you, Deryn.

ZOË SKOULDING

Zoë Skoulding has published four full-length collections of poetry: *Tide Table* (Gwasg Pantycelyn, 1998); *The Mirror Trade* (Seren, 2004), *Remains of a Future City* (Seren, 2008), and *The Museum of Disappearing Sounds* (Seren, 2013). She co-authored *Dark Wires* with Ian Davidson (West House Books, 2007); *From Here* with Simonetta Moro (Dusie, 2008) and *Metropoetica – Poetry and urban space:Women writing cities* with Ingmāra Balode, Julia Fiedorczuk, Sanna Karlström, Ana Pepelnik, Sigurbjörg Þrastardóttir and Elżbieta Wójcik-Leese (Seren, 2103). Her translations include *In Reality: Selected Poems* (Seren, 2013) from the French of Jean Portante. Critical works include *Placing Poetry*, co-edited with Ian Davidson (Rodopi, 2013) and the monograph *Contemporary Women's Poetry and Urban Space: Experimental Cities* (Palgrave Macmillan, 2013). She is a member of the sound art collective Parking Non-Stop, founded the little poetry magazine in 1994, and edited from 2008-2014. She lives in Bangor, and lectures in Creative Writing at Bangor University.

Can we start with Remains of a Future City? *I know it draws on the ideas of Guy Debord and the Situationist movement which emerged in Paris in the fifties. Did the book develop out of your interest in the movement or were you already thinking about cities?*
I was already thinking about city space, and then I read *Formulary for A New Urbanism*, a Situationist manifesto from the fifties by the then nineteen-year-old Ivan Chtcheglov – which extends psychoanalysis into the architecture of the city with a

certain utopian optimism. He describes moving through different quarters that would generate particular states of mind, but although he is clearly drawing on Paris, it's an imaginary architecture rather than a specific urban environment. Situationism emphasised the experience of daily life rather than the abstracted and reified work of art, but what we're left with, paradoxically, is his very poetic text. Situationism grew out of Dada's anti-art approaches, so the 'Situationist poem' is a contradiction in terms – and one I played with deliberately. The first poems I wrote took phrases from his text as titles, like 'The House Where It Is Impossible Not to Fall in Love' or 'The Noble and Tragic Quarter', which I liked for their exaggerated artifice. The process of writing involved building one text over another, like the house of the architect Frank Gehry, that encases an old building in new structures and materials.

Were you consciously researching architecture?
I was at the time, but it had been an interest since 'A' level art history and I also did a module on American architecture as part of my English degree at Exeter. *Remains* grew out of a set of ideas I'd worked through in *The Mirror Trade*. The Canadian poet Lisa Robertson's work on architecture (for example in *Occasional Work* and *Seven Walks from the Office of Soft Architecture*) led me to Rem Koolhaas's *Delirious New York*, and Elizabeth Grosz's *Architecture from the Outside*, among other things.

The poems seem to me to build and dismantle themselves at the same time, and quite playfully. Like they're mocking history, or historicity?
In the fifties, Chtcheglov was projecting into a future that's now the past. Despite the playfulness and irony in his text, I don't think it's possible to inhabit that kind of utopian vision now. So yes, that tension between a past looking forward and a future looking back intrigues me, along with the instability that comes from looking backwards and forwards at the same time. I'm as interested in time as I am in space; I don't think the two are separable.

The whole collection seems to challenge the fixing of things – tempo-rally, spatially and for me even expressively: anything I might say about it seems to risk over-determining it. The whole book seems permeable, so the poems seem full of spaces, even if they're often about structures.

I was interested in structures being half-built or falling down. That's what a city is and perhaps also what ideas are. The word 'city' suggests some kind of total structure: Chtcheglov has in mind a complete entity, and there are many similar visions from earlier periods, Tommaso Campanella's *City of the Sun* for example. There's an allegorical structure in that sort of organis-ing of space – I'm thinking of Borges, or Calvino's *Invisible Cities*, or even Dante's *Divine Comedy*. There's a whole lineage of imagi-native structures evoked in the idea of the city, but they're problematic because the individual always has a particular relationship with any overarching structure. The person who's articulated that best for me is Michel de Certeau, in his essay 'Walking in the City'[1]. As I was writing, I was thinking about the concept of the city but also the idea of walking and inhabiting it from different perspectives. I wanted to see how far the text itself might create ways of moving through a space, like Walter Benjamin's *The Arcades Project*[2], which was another important text for me. I wanted forms that would allow me to create the same kind of movement. I was thinking in quite a visual way: moving around a city where different parts of it would have different shapes – for example there would be a tower-shaped tower, and a castle, with crenellations. I wanted every poem to be a distinct place but also for there to be spaces in the poems to move through. The broken lines and their spacing refer back to the American poet Charles Olson and open field poetry.

And William Carlos Williams?
Yes, in fact probably Williams' *Paterson* was a more significant influence on its form, now I think about it. But I didn't want to be consistent about any of this. The degrees of disruption in syntax and form differ from poem to poem just as different architectural styles co-exist in a city. I like the juxtaposition of old and new.

I was struck by how urban and rural seem steeped in each other somehow, and yet the more entangled they come to seem, the more alien also...

The city – or the building site – is permeated by the natural world. Although I was trying to write about a city, the poems kept drawing me back to the rural. I was interested in those distinctions. What does 'urban' mean? But it's also to do with orienting myself, seeing where I am and thinking about what it means to be in the city. How does what I'm doing relate to, say, the European city? Well I am in a European city – Bangor – but I also live just outside it. There's a CCTV camera on Menai Bridge that projects footage of the bridge which friends in America watch occasionally; it's on the BBC website. So this is hardly a remote or unspoiled rural experience! I often walk along a footpath along the Menai Straits between the two bridges and it's always reminded me of Berlin. My poem 'The Bridge' came out of walking round lost areas of Berlin where the Wall had been dismantled and the trees cut down: it was urban space that had become forest, and the trees were there because of a political event. The place intrigued me because it made those connections so visible. Down by the Straits, you can be walking under the Britannia Bridge with traffic above you going somewhere else, and yet you're on a woodland path. The two contexts intersect in a cultural-ecological space.

This is ecology as network, or at least as a culturally networked space. Has it got edges?

I guess not, but this would be a way of thinking about any space, wouldn't it, in terms of network and the interconnection between local and global? An ecological sensibility might just be one aspect of that, albeit an important one.

I can't help reading ruination into Remains, *although you call Chtcheglov an optimist. In places your vision seems profoundly pessimistic, more dystopian than utopian. Is that fair?*

For me the poems exist as possibilities of something that will never be completed, and that's about as optimistic as I get. In *Far*

Language[3] Robert Sheppard writes about having utopian ideas, but shattered and broken ones – partial or incomplete utopias. There are different ways of looking at fragmentation aren't there? If modernist fragmentation refers back to a lost wholeness, there's also a more postmodern view of continuous fragmentation and rhizomatic regrowth. I draw on both; I'm looking back to those ideas of modernist loss while trying to place them in a continuous process. Perhaps...

Is that a way of explaining your work overall? I'm thinking about how you use form, and its relation to textuality
It's more a continuous negotiation of where I am, through language and how I understand it. A Danish poet I very much admire, Morten Søndergaard, has said that writing poetry is like a bat squeaking, sending out signals to see what bounces back. I liked that description. Probably that wasn't how I started writing but increasingly that's what I'm moving towards or that's what I want it to be.

How did you start writing?
I went to north India in 1990 to teach at an international school after finishing my degree. I'd been a keen reader of poetry but hadn't really thought I'd write it. I was more interested in visual art. I started writing partly because of the shock of being in a completely new context. My late father was born in India, which made me question the nature of my relationship with this place, which was deep and complicated, given its colonial history. I also developed a certain ecological interest from walking in the Himalayan foothills where I was living. Flooding and deforestation were all too evident, but there was also a scale and wildness I had never encountered before. I started writing in response. I went from there to Bangor to train as a teacher and then taught secondary English from 1992 to 2004. Encouraging children to write poetry was also a way of teaching myself. The literature syllabus (particularly for the WJEC, influenced by Sandra Anstey who'd worked previously at *Poetry Wales*) introduced me very quickly to a Welsh context, and I worked with an inspirational

Head of Department, Mel Jones, who introduced me to new Welsh poetry in English. He was a poet himself, although he kept it quiet. At the same time, the job was gruelling, so I was writing with desperate energy at weekends to prove to myself that I still had a life outside it.

India to Bangor – quite a leap. Did North Wales make you welcome?
It was a very exciting time. My social connections were mainly through music in the 1990s – I shared a house with Owain Wright of Rheinallt H. Rowlands, and occasionally wrote lyrics for him, and then for David Wrench, with whom I was briefly in a group playing bass. Other friends included Ectogram, my husband Alan Holmes' band, and Gorky's Zygotic Mynci, who recorded near us when Alan was their producer. There was a very vibrant music scene across both languages, encouraged partly by S4C programming. But I didn't know many writers, so I started the little magazine *Skald* in 1994 to try and create a community because I didn't have one as a writer. I wanted it to work bilingually – to have a Welsh-speaking co-editor – but despite the best efforts of Maldwyn Thomas in the first couple of years it remained a mainly English-language publication.

It was a bold thing to do…
Well, I remember I sent a handwritten letter to Tony Bianchi at the Arts Council of Wales with the first copy. Miraculously, it seemed to me then, he offered me funding for subsequent issues. It wasn't much money at all but it meant a lot to be trusted and encouraged in that way. Co-editing the magazine from 2002 with Ian Davidson was very interesting because its scope widened beyond Wales to include more experimental and international work.

It all sounds very stimulating and hospitable. Would you construct Wales in that way? How do you think of Wales?
Yes, it's been hospitable. I've always been aware of people actively trying to build and sustain an independent Welsh culture. Robert Minhinnick's support of younger writers in *Poetry Wales* was part of that and I tried to follow his example. At the same time, living

in Bangor and not being Welsh-speaking to any useful extent (despite numerous courses!) has created an interesting situation for me. I'll always be an outsider in some ways, but that in itself has given me a productive tension to work in and around.

You didn't need to speak Welsh to share in the energy?
At the time I arrived there was a real energy around music that was connected with the Welsh language community, but it wasn't at all exclusive. It seemed exciting that this music scene had evolved outside London, in north Wales. There was a set of coordinates that covered Wales, connecting Bangor with Cardiff, but also reaching outwards to Europe, where several of these groups had played extensively and found sympathetic networks. So there was a sense of north Wales being isolated in the UK but because of that able to make different kinds of connections. I had moved there just before 1992 and all the changes in Europe, so I was hopeful that Wales would find a new independent role in that context.

Europe is such an important part of your work. I'm thinking of Metropoetica. *Can you tell me a bit about that project?*
Metropoetica was a collaboration between women poets in European cities between 2009 and 2011, organised with Literature Across Frontiers. The aim was to place the activities of writing poetry and translating it within the lived context of the city. We held workshops in Krakow, Ljubljana, Riga, Wroclaw and Athens, and worked together online. One activity, even before we had met face to face, was to look at online maps and make a set of directions for one of the other poets to follow in her own city. She would walk the route, write about it, and then the resulting text would be translated, so there were translations between virtual and 'real' spaces as well as between different languages. The collaborative aspect was very important, and it came from what I was saying earlier: that the city cannot be adequately represented from a single viewpoint – it's always about plurality.

Did you enjoy the project? Was it hard to work across that geography?
It was wonderful to work with the others and to develop longer

exchanges than usually happens at a literary festival or translation workshop. Most of us are still in touch, so in some ways the
project isn't over. I've really appreciated the work of Literature
Across Frontiers in bringing writers together in very productive
ways during that period. Each time we met we were working
under pressure to produce a performance or output of some
kind; looking back I'm amazed at what we achieved. The
thematic approach allowed us to work at speed and we could
draw on existing shared interests, because we were all already
engaged with city space in various ways. But we were also trying
to respond to entirely new urban environments in a very short
space of time – sometimes too quickly, I felt. It raised questions
about the representation of place that perhaps we didn't fully
resolve, but which have become important to me subsequently,
so it was all worth trying out. The other strand of the project was
based on poet-to-poet translation without knowledge of the
source language. It's a fascinating process and an important one
for smaller languages: so, Icelandic poems were translated into
Latvian, or Polish ones into Finnish. We also experimented with
homophonic translation, and with leaving words untranslated. It
all opened up to me the immense creative possibilities of translation. It also made me want to discover what it's like to translate
without being dependent on the poet's own interpretation of
their work, so over the last few years I've been re-learning French
and appreciating the ways in which another language gives my
English a different space to breathe in.

*We're back to Europe again. Where does your interest in Europe spring
from?*
When I was seventeen I went to live in Belgium – the Flemish part
– to learn French with a French-speaking family. That was my
introduction to bilingual complexity. I've quite often gone back to
Brussels, with the increasing sense that the European Union is also
a utopian project, with its attendant problems and failures. But I'm
still convinced that Europe is Wales's best hope, and absolutely
fundamental to its devolution. The island mentality that pervades
the UK is very depressing, and while we can't do anything about

our location we don't need to be part of that thinking.

It's not just Belgium, or Paris, there's Prague and Berlin and other Eastern European centres, or places...
I'm sometimes quite deliberately writing Wales into a broader European context in order to make sense of my place in it, and of the tensions that exist around me. The Montreal poet Erin Mouré's book poem *Cidadán* (House of Anansi, 2002) talks about how a national determination within a larger framework (like Quebec in Canada) creates a kind of edge: a cultural ambiguity which is also a moment of freedom. I think it's along those edges, those fault lines, that you get something interesting happening. And of course we have that in Wales, that line, along language and perhaps other geographical lines too, and if you connect those lines within the much more complex picture of Europe then they become part of something else. It avoids the binaries that trap us in Wales, the sense of being up against one particular edge: it puts you in a context where there are multiple edges, which are always moving.

Can we talk about your 'I'? Your handling of place/experience has been informed by psycho-geographic practice, but your poems hardly ever sound personal. Are you ever your own subject?
I've been thinking about that 'I' while rereading and revising this interview, which we began face to face in Cardiff in 2008. The process of updating it has made me aware of how my view of my life and work has shifted since then. What we're making now, and what the reader will encounter, is a palimpsest of the two versions of Zoë Skoulding. Obviously she's invented because even I don't know which one she is; I suspect she's not quite either of them. On the other hand, I try to be as truthful as possible in my poems. All my poems are based on real experience, and are driven by emotion that pushes me into thinking, but then again they happen in language, which always involves fiction.

The process of writing, let's say those poems, also of course presumes, depends, on there being someone out there to read them, and engage

*with the experiences of that truthful Zoë. Do you ever imagine that
reader, or think about their relationship with the text?*
I think that relationship's out of my control. I think it's my job as
a writer to work as honestly as I can with what I've got and then
leave it. So I don't have a specific idea of a projected reader; I just
assume that if I make something I'd want to read, then someone
else would want to read it too.

*Perhaps because in Wales the poet belongs to a particular social
history, I can't help but think of you as a political poet, speaking to
and about the ways different groups of people construct or identify
with Wales.*
I would hope I am political, although I'm generally more interested in the creation of tentative alternative possibilities than in
direct statement. The priest-poet and the teacher-poet are familiar roles in Welsh poetry, and having been both a vicar's daughter
and teacher, I recoil from both. I don't want to exert rhetorical
power over a reader so I want the text to be a shared environment. I like to think in terms of making a structure that I can
inhabit, because if I can live in it someone else can too. My work
engages with public space, which is always a political concern,
but I approach it through my own perceptions and experience,
which are also political. Nothing isn't! So if mapping poems like
'Forest with A to Z of Cardiff' (*Remains*) ask questions about
who describes or controls the space we're in and how it's represented, more recent work thinks about the poem itself as a place
made of sound, often opaque and echoing, that contrasts with the
stream of images selling us the world on our computer screens.

*So you conceive of the poem as having political power, political
agency?*
Well, this comes back to the conundrum of the Situationists; to
that view of the lived experience versus art. I am interested in
social space, and yet the experience of writing about it is quite
private, as is the reader's. So what effect does – can – writing have
in a public domain? We're back to that question of optimism: the
space made in a book is a small one but it's nevertheless a

material space in which something can change. If it's poetry, relatively few people will encounter it and it might not change much – but it's better than nothing.

So you can only ever assume so much of what you're making? That makes it a collective enterprise...
Absolutely, and that's there in the form, too; there are ambiguities of syntax that require the reader to enter that space and do something with it. Other poets do this to a greater degree than I do but yes, I'd see the reader as completing or participating in that. There's not really much of an 'I' in the poems; it's flickering around between pronouns quite often. And there aren't many individual people in the poems, either, but there is a sense of a collective – architecture becomes a way of talking about shared space, so community is implicit.

Perhaps we could say that there's an 'eye' instead, looking? And it's mobile, forever shifting about. Would you gender it?
I'm aware of that movement and, yes, I think there is a relationship between shifting perspective and gender, although obviously not in terms of a simple opposition between male and female writers. Denise Riley, in both her theoretical work and her poetry, shows how the identification 'women' is inhabited differently at different times. I pick this up in my monograph, which explores how a range of women poets write about the city. So, there's the use of pronouns in, say, Lisa Robertson's manifesto-like 'we', or in Lisa Samuels' *Gender City* (Shearsman, 2011), where they create a particular collective vision. Geraldine Monk's 'I' in *Escafeld Hangings* (West House, 2005) is made up of multiple voices switching between historical periods, while Erin Mouré and Agnes Lehóczky work across linguistic boundaries in urban space. In Alice Notley's work, the underground describes a space of dissent, but in a fusing of speech and perception so fast that we're always on the move.

You call these poets 'experimental'. Why not, say, 'innovative' (Maggie O'Sullivan's choice for her anthology Out of Everywhere) *or*

'radical' (which Harriet Tarlo uses for hers, The Ground Aslant)?
'Innovative' is too much used in promotional writing. It stresses
novelty, which isn't the point. I prefer 'radical' and I like the way
Harriet uses it in her anthology (in which I'm very pleased to be
included). But 'radical' can imply a more direct political aim, an
action of going back to the roots, which doesn't quite work for
me; it doesn't seem fair to expect poetry to live up to that,
whereas 'experimental' is interestingly linked with 'experience',
and holds slightly contradictory meanings implying both a rigor-
ously applied process and spontaneous or speculative
approaches to writing.

Would you want your own writing to be thought of as experimental?
Yes. It didn't start that way but increasingly it's become so. The
reading that's been most important to me has certainly been in
that area, though the writerly networks which often define UK
experimental poetry are predominantly English, albeit with links
to the US and Europe. The fact that I fall somewhere between
those networks and the Welsh context, in which I'm also partly an
outsider, is probably another reason for my identification with
European poetry.

*Collaboration is another way of complicating the singular-seeming
author. You've done a fair bit of collaborative work. Did it start with
Ian Davidson?*
Yes, I met Ian at Bangor in 2001. We were both doing PhDs at
the time. I was trying to apply postcolonial thinking to Wales in
terms of place and identity, and Ian was writing on space in
contemporary poetry. We had some shared interests and his work
opened up a lot of new thinking and, importantly, new reading,
at just the right time. I asked him to co-edit *Skald* with me and
we went on to write collaboratively together. For about two years,
from 2003 to 2005, we emailed each other four lines of poetry
twice a week, and some of the results appeared in *Dark Wires*.

*So with Ian and people like the New York artist Simonetta Moro, and
through* Metropoetica, *you've co-written essays, co-authored – or co-*

produced – collections, co-edited an anthology of critical essays. What attracts about collaboration?

With Simonetta, the translation was between visual and verbal; she sent me drawings and I responded with a poem each time. It was a fascinating way of thinking about the differences between image and word. We'd only met briefly at a conference, and we didn't discuss the work while it was in progress, so the collaboration was itself the conversation. With Ian, too, the poems existed in their own space and we didn't discuss them until they were finished. After we'd finished, we often couldn't remember who had written what, but we could see the words for what they were; we became our own readers as well as writers. This distancing of the self is also very much part of translation: whose poem is it, when the sounds are all in another language? Yes there are losses, but language, which is our medium as writers, can begin to reveal its own surprises.

Going back to the bat and its signals, your latest collection The Museum of Disappearing Sounds *asks me to somehow visualise, or perhaps try to give shape to, the sounds which a poem enshrines; to allow it to sound itself, as it were. It reminds me of the way* Remains of a Future City *asks me to 'see' a temporally impossible space, a future imagined from the past...*

The collection starts from a question asked by the Canadian composer and sound ecologist R. Murray Schafer: 'Where are the museums for disappearing sounds?' Schafer's work is to do with valuing the traditional rhythms and sound patterns of particular communities as they are being erased by the continuous noise of industrialisation. My own work has evolved within a set of interests in which noise – the noise of others – is a central concern. I write in English in a bilingual community, where my English speech is the noise that Welsh-speakers may want to filter out. My understanding of Welsh is partial, therefore I hear Welsh partly as sound, as noise perhaps, but noise that's a welcome aspect of my sound environment, important in the way I live alongside friends and neighbours. I'm still closely involved with music. I sometimes perform my work in a particular sound context, often using electronic effects to make a textural backdrop for the voice, to take it away from being just mine and foreground its relationship to an environment of physical sound. I also work with Alan, who sometimes performs soundscapes – collages of field recordings – along with my poems. My title poem dramatizes Murray Schafer's image of the Museum – but of course recording technology turns the computer into a repository for all the sounds that happened once in the real world; it can store, rearrange and recontextualise them. Which is what writing does, incompletely, to the voice: traps it in time outside the social rhythm of speech, and fundamentally alters it at the same time. There's a visual aspect to all this, in the poem's shape on the page, which I think of as a negotiation with silence. Silence in a Cagean sense, which isn't silent: it's a space for someone else's perspective to come through, for other lives to exist.

Can we finish with Poetry Wales. *Did you enjoy that job? Do you think it's left any effect on your own writing?*
I enjoyed the editorship very much. I had a strong sense of magazine's past and felt that I was continuing a path, particularly with international connections, that had been opened up by Robert Minhinnick before me. I was more interested in experimental work than earlier editors, but there's less of it in Wales than one might expect, possibly because Wales's histories of language and dissent have their own particular contours. It was exciting nevertheless to bring some different voices into those dialogues. The editorship sharpened my interest in translation, which has become an increasingly integral part of my writing practice. It gave me more to draw on, in terms of thinking about what a poem can be, through close encounters with other languages and their poetic traditions. It's left me more confident in the originality of translation; thinking of all writing as translation of one kind or another, and of the provisionality of writing; like the translation, the poem is one version among many possibilities. It leaves space for all the others to come.

Many thanks, Zoë.

1. Michel de Certeau, *The Practice of Everyday Life*, trans. Steven Rendall, 1984.
2. Walter Benjamin, *The Arcades Project*, trans. Howard Eiland and Kevin McLaughlin, Cambridge MA : Havard University Press, 1999.
3. Robert Sheppard, *Far Language*, Exeter: Stride, 1999.

ANNE STEVENSON

Anne Stevenson has published fifteen collections of poetry in the UK: *Travelling Behind Glass: Selected Poems 1963-1973* (Oxford, 1974); *Correspondences: A Family History in Letters* (Oxford, 1974); *Enough of Green* (Oxford, 1977); *Sonnets for Five Seasons* (Five Seasons, 1979); *Minute by Glass Minute* (Oxford, 1982); *A Legacy* (Taxvs, 1983); *The Fiction-makers* (Oxford, 1985); *Selected Poems 1956-1986* (Oxford, 1987); *The Other House* (Oxford, 1990); *Four and a Half Dancing Men* (Oxford, 1993); *Granny Scarecrow* (Bloodaxe, 2000); *A Report from the Border* (Bloodaxe, 2003); *Poems 1955-2005* (Bloodaxe, 2006); *Stone Milk* (Bloodaxe, 2007) and *Astonishment* (Bloodaxe, 2012). *Selected Poems* (Library of Anerica) appeared in 2008. She has worked in many universities, and has authored various critical works, including *Elizabeth Bishop* (Twayne, 1966); *Bitter Fame: A Life of Sylvia Plath* (Viking, 1989); and *Five Looks at Elizabeth Bishop* (Bloodaxe, 2006). A selection of her critical essays can be found in *Between the Iceberg and the Ship* (University of Michigan, 1998). She divides her time between her home in County Durham and a remote cottage in Ardudwy, Gwynedd. This interview was conducted entirely by email. It had hardly begun when news broke of Nobel Laureate Seamus Heaney's unexpected death at the age of 74.

I know you knew Seamus Heaney personally. Were you good friends?
I met Seamus in the early seventies when I visited him and Maire in Wicklow with Philip Hobsbaum. My two sons were maybe six and seven – close to the age of their two boys. We explored the coast with the children and did some pub-crawling, and talked

about poetry. Seamus had just written a poem that combined the theme of an embryo's first stirrings in the womb (Maire was pregnant with their daughter Catherine) and the colonial relationship of Ireland with England. It occurred either to me or Philip that a good title would be 'Act of Union'. (I remember it as my idea, though it may have been Philip's.) In January 1977 Heaney and Ted Hughes were guests of a poetry group I'd started in Oxford. I introduced them when they read together in a huge crowded hall.

Heaney was for me, above all, a poet of the right angle and the right words for his time and place. He was beyond question the right poet for Ireland; called into being by 'The Troubles', but able to speak through them to both factions. He spoke lovingly always to and for people of his own kind. The whole population, North and South, knew and loved him. It has always surprised me, though, that he has been so popular in England and America, for his best work isn't easy for outsiders to grasp. I suppose it was his translucent friendliness and honesty that people admired. He had an open, natural, earthbound personality suited to winning all the prizes. He deserved them.

You're very different writers. Would you say you had common poetic interests? Are you aware of having learned anything from him, perhaps?
I can't say I learned much about writing poetry from Heaney; I was the elder when we met, and we came from diametrically different backgrounds. He was a Catholic farmer's son, chosen out of his family for a thoroughly Catholic education; he seems never to have deviated from the academic high road his education opened before him. As he rose in his profession, he succeeded wonderfully in his private life: one good, faithful wife all his life, three children, universal fame, happily ever after until he was felled by his first stroke a few years ago. Whereas I am a Protestant American woman, oldest daughter of an atheist Professor of Philosophy, brought up in the academic atmosphere of Harvard, Yale and The University of Michigan. As a child, I took it for granted that my house would be full of books and that

I would read many of them, that my father would own two grand pianos on which I would learn to play, that music was Bach, Mozart and Beethoven, and that literature was Shakespeare, Keats and Jane Austen.

Then, of course, I rebelled. After graduating, I decided to leave academia forever by marrying an adventuresome Englishman. Divorced seven years later, after moving with the Englishman from Cambridge to London to Belfast to New York to Mississippi and Georgia in the American South, I shame-facedly returned to Michigan with a three-year-old daughter to take an MA in English. Then, after school teaching in Massachusetts, I married a second Englishman – a Sinologist, and now a well-known historian – and produced two sons born in Cambridge and Glasgow. Divorced again in Oxford, I pursued a mad course in Hay-on-Wye, London, Edinburgh, Cambridge, Durham, North Wales and finally Durham again. My poems were almost all written in a search for something that was not sex, not family, not status, not an 'identity', not a religious or political or philosophical belief; something that a very early poem, 'New York', stumbles on: 'As if love, love, love were the only green in the jungle.' When in the 1960s I read and later corresponded with Elizabeth Bishop, I realised that, likewise for her 'something, something, something' was somehow terribly important, something that neither she nor I could long hold in focus. Love? Beauty? Truth? Until I married Peter Lucas in London in 1987, I never really settled happily anywhere with anyone.

Heaney never lets us forget about the labour of writing a poem. I've always admired that; I've little patience with the idea of 'inspiration'. I am (and Heaney would have been) sympathetic to your suspicion of 'inspiration'; poems for me are the proverbial 99% perspiration, but I need a 'tune' to get started, a phrase without words at first, as Mandelstam had it, a cadence humming in the ears. As Nadezhda Mandelstam's *Hope Against Hope* describes it:

> It begins with a musical phrase ringing insistently in the ears; at first inchoate, it later takes on a precise form,

though still without words. I sometimes saw M trying to get rid of this kind of 'hum', to brush it off and escape from it. He would toss his head as though it could be shaken out like a drop of water that gets into your ear while bathing. But it was always louder than any noise, radio or conversation in the room...

That has been my experience of receiving poetry since I was a small child.

I don't think anyone reading your poems could overlook the importance of music to your work. Would you have rather been a musician?
The simple answer is no. I never was a good enough cellist or pianist to be more than an amateur. As a child I fantasised about becoming a 'great' composer like Mozart, a 'great' actress like Katherine Cornell, a 'great' novelist like Jane Austen or Tolstoy. But I knew even as a teenager that the only gift I could lay claim to was for writing poems.

What about philosophy? I've realised that I think of you as being something of a philosopher, perhaps because of your father.
From my father I learned much more about music and poetry (and music in poetry) than I ever did about philosophy, which I never studied seriously. My affiliations lie, like his, with Lucretius and David Hume, not with Platonic Idealists or metaphysicians, nor with the existentialists. As a young woman, I suppose I indulged in romantic fantasies while never really believing in them. Deep down, I've always been a pragmatist with a deep respect for science, suspicious of religion, though during one marriage I tried hard to adapt to Christian belief. When I became deaf at about 30, I gave up music; it was too painful to listen to 'so many nails falling into a bucket', as my deaf youngest sister put it. I now hear with the help of a cochlear implant and a fancy digital hearing aid, which, between them, help me to hear myself on the piano. But I play only to myself, and always music I remember from the days when I could hear normally.

I hadn't realised that you lost your hearing so young. That must have been grim. Did it make much of an impact on your writing at the time?

Don't feel too sorry for me. My deafness came on gradually when I was in my 20s and I adjusted to it, learning how to hear with my inner ear, as it were. Which was all I needed for the rhythms that came to me as poems. In some ways it was a relief to lose all ambition in music, excessive ambition being one of the traits I most dislike about myself. A little quatrain, written five or six years ago, says it all. 'I've lost a sense, why should I care? / Searching myself I find a spare. / I keep that sixth sense in repair / And set it deftly, like a snare.'

Perhaps we could revisit the fantasy? You've written in poetry and prose about some of the frustrations and difficulties which you experienced as a young wife and mother.

I can't blame literature for my failings as a wife and mother. I suppose I look back now with some understanding to the in-between era I stumbled into when I left America under the impression that England would provide me with the culture Henry James, for example, anticipated would collapse after the First World War and which writers like Evelyn Waugh saw off for good in the aftermath of the Second. Since then, 'high culture' has had to fight to hold its head up before a mass audience antagonistic to 'elitism', who bad-mouth good taste in the name of pluralist democracy. The novelist, John Fowles put his finger on the difficulty when he quoted from Antonio Gramsci's *Prison Notebooks*: 'The crisis consists precisely in the fact that the old is dying and the new cannot be born; in this inter-regnum a great variety of morbid symptoms appears.' Chief among these symptoms still seems to be, in the West, selfish individualism, uncontrolled consumerism, a sacrifice of community, a sacrifice of natural beauty, the dumbing down of higher education and the exploitation and cheapening of art. In our new, in many ways more charitable, ethnically mixed global society, what passes for egalitarian culture is everywhere supported by capitalistic enterprise and competition – not least by the celebrity worship and self-presentation that has produced Facebook, Twitter and ever-smarter phones.

Would you say that culture is patriarchal?
Well yes, what you call 'patriarchy' in Britain has exploited women in the past and I believe sneakily still does. I have to say, though, that after I was first married in England I got a job as an 'Advertising Manager' with an established London publisher on the strength of being an American woman who must know all about such un-English matters. In America, middle-class educated women have even been spoiled. In New Haven during the war, my father, hardly a patriarchal tyrant, supported seven women on an assistant professor's salary: my mother, her mother, my sister, myself, two English girls, refugees from Cambridge plus an Irish maid (sometimes two) employed out of charity because patriotic families in New Haven refused to hire people from neutral Ireland. During my early years in England, I was too dazed to be aware either of class or gender prejudices. Like many young women at the time, I cast myself as the heroine of my own Margaret Drabble novel, the clever, observant wife of an ambitious husband. He made the money. I took care of the house and babies. Only later did I find myself, to my amazement, lonely, benumbed, unfulfilled, frustrated and difficult to live with. I didn't adapt well to motherhood. We moved around too much to make compatible friends, and selfishly, I wanted unlimited time to read and write. Yet, when I did get jobs or signed up for various university courses, not one of my husbands ever objected. Perhaps we shouldn't generalise. If I hadn't valued poetry and music above domestic happiness I would never have made myself so miserable.

Looking back, what might you say to a younger you? Is there no way of reconciling writing with family life? Must it be different for women?
Reconciling family life with a compulsion to engage with any intellectual or creative challenge is extremely difficult – even today, particularly difficult for women. The pressures on me were set by precedent (my mother, my grandmother), by social

conscience ('When a woman enters a room full of guests she should make everyone feel happier for her being there') and by a combination of selfishness, self-doubt and laziness. I'd warn my younger self that giving her life to her art would mean making some serious choices, first among them, whether to marry and risk children. Until recently, women writers were mostly by choice or fate single, or became honorary men and remained childless. I think of Jane Austen, George Eliot, the Bronte sisters, Charlotte Mew, Virginia Woolf, Marianne Moore, Stevie Smith, Elizabeth Bishop. For normal women at twenty the sexual instinct is very strong, as it was with Sylvia Plath and the generation of college-educated women born in the 1930s. Most of us fell into marriage as easily as we fell into bed. We had babies in our twenties and were content until we realised that taking responsibility for a fresh generation meant that we had more or less to march down the hill of our ambition to carry our children up hills of their own. We didn't anticipate a time in our late forties and fifties when we might have a chance to find ourselves again, with children and grandchildren fulfilling an important part of our understanding; we couldn't see that far ahead. So, many of us (including myself) were first miserable and then defiant. Hence the origin of the Women's Movement and Feminism as we know it now.

You didn't turn to the Women's movement for help or companionship, did you? Many poets shrug off the label of 'feminist' poet. Would you go as far as saying that feminism was bad for literature?
I suspect that feminism hasn't been very good for poetry, however spiritually sustaining for certain kinds of women. I'm suspicious of isms of any kind, including what I think of as *genderism* in literature. 'Emotion is a rotten base for politics' (that's a quote from a Dick Francis thriller) but surely emotion is the common psychological base from which poetry begins to engage with imaginative truth and insight. Poetry has to discipline its breaking with political conformities. The more original or surprising its discoveries, the more rhythms and distancing metaphors should help check its slide into self-interest. In the

kind of poetry I associate with women's consciousness raising groups the emphasis is all on what their poems have to say, not on how language can delight in its own music, contradict itself, play with ideas on several levels, or teach the poet something s/he didn't know before s/he began to write. 'A poem begins in delight and ends in wisdom,' wrote Robert Frost. Or to borrow Heaney's image, a poet digs with his pen to uncover a story or a history that is there for us all, not just for the poet's personal satisfaction of confessing sins or justifying some shocking or unpalatable behaviour.

I'm not saying, of course, that politics is not a huge emotional factor in many poets' lives. What worries me is that political poetry of any kind too easily puts on the lineaments of propaganda. A poem that begins by defining or defending a cause – even if it is a just cause – is likely to fail for lack of a living dimension, of a poet feeling out for something he doesn't yet fully understand.

We started by talking about Seamus Heaney, but you wouldn't have been reading him when you first started writing. Which poets did you read early on?
The poets after whose work I modelled my early poems, (still do, I suppose) would have to have been Shakespeare, his lyrics and sonnets particularly; then John Donne and Andrew Marvell. I fell in love with Keats and Byron, and with Wordsworth's sonnets, but never took to Shelley. In high school I learned a lot of Robert Frost by heart and imitated Emily Dickinson, to whose work I was slower to warm. I wrote ballads like Walter Scott and copied Browning's dramatic monologues. I liked Yeats, I think, purely for the sound of his poems as recited by my father, who preferred his Irish madness to the Christian preaching of T.S. Eliot. Later I became a 'modernist' after Eliot and Pound, Auden and Wallace Stevens. Marianne Moore I liked very much, Thomas Hardy, too, and William Carlos Williams and Randall Jarrell's criticism. It wasn't until 1960 that I read Elizabeth Bishop, whose sane and beautiful poems were a revelation to me in that frantic decade, saving me from Sylvia Plath's siren songs.

'Siren songs' – that's interesting. So many women writers have said
something similar about Plath. You've written critically on Plath; I
hadn't realised she'd felt dangerous to you, too.
I think Plath was a problem from the time I first read *Ariel* in
1965. At first I felt awe. How had she managed to write poems
so powerfully expressive of the angst many American women-
graduates felt in that time-chasm between an out of date social
pattern and an inchoate new one? Plath died before the women's
movement got under way, but her poems catapulted many
discontented women into it; and if, like me, you didn't want to
join the movement (or any movement) you felt excluded from
the inevitable. Was I moved to write on Plath because I was
jealous of her, as many reviewers of *Bitter Fame* concluded? I
don't think so. On reflection, I believe – as I've said elsewhere –
that Sylvia Plath was a victim of her own brilliantly imaginative
brain, which was probably irrevocably damaged when, in the
summer of 1953, sleepless and fearful of going mad, she was
given, as an outpatient, electroconvulsive therapy (ECT) by a
careless and incompetent psychiatrist in a run-of-the-mill
Massachusetts mental hospital. In this, I believe, she was tragically a victim of a time when ECT was considered an efficient
and effective psychoanalytical practice. There is little doubt that
Plath's treatment by electrolysis led directly to her first suicide
attempt. My guess is that, for the rest of her life, suicide remained
for her a solution to unbearable personal anguish, a challenge
unsuccessfully attempted once, so maybe still a possible release
into a better life, or even an afterlife. This is clear from the
remarks she made to her downstairs neighbour, Professor
Thomas, the night before she died, paying him for postage
stamps then and there, 'or I won't be right with my conscience
before God.'

You once wondered out loud (to Richard Poole) whether you weren't a
true puritan. Was that to do with faith/religion, or cultural origins? I
found myself musing on whether you'd have gone on the Mayflower…
I don't know about the Mayflower. I suspect that, though a
dissenter, I would have opted not to join the group for its

religious orthodoxy. I don't know why I ever told Richard Poole that I was a puritan (with a lower case 'p') unless, like Plath, I felt wounded in my ego. Now I think about it, 'wounded puritan' might describe me. I certainly felt wounded after *Bitter Fame* attracted so many unfriendly reviews. And I still feel that the poems I have written lately, with their Darwinian perspective and attention to cogent argument and poetic form, are passed over by a poetry establishment that chiefly prizes verbal novelty or popular taste.

I was interested to hear you identifying Donne and Marvell earlier, because like the so-called Metaphysical poets, in your poems, nothing is ever simply decorative. Images, music and so on always help reveal or explain an idea or an association.

I hope so, yes. I don't often write a poem without wanting to make some kind of discovery or engage with some insight or idea.

Rereading your collections, I've been struck by how far a single poem can travel; there's a kind of voracity about your writing. And something self-entertaining about your use of form.

I agree with all that. In the years after the breakdown of my first marriage, I decided – solely on the basis of observation – that most people I knew were either play-acting in their social relationships or playing games. Writing a poem, I suppose, partakes of both, although at the same time a poem is seeing through its own act and its own game. Elizabeth Bishop pointed out that though writing a poem was an entirely unnatural act, the art of it was to make it sound as natural as possible. As Eliot says, 'Human kind cannot bear very much reality.' So theatricality seems to me praiseworthy in poetry so long as it's distanced and looks with some detachment at the whole of the human comedy/ tragedy, not just at one poet's little life and desires. For all Plath's gifts and valiant struggle, she never was able to free herself from herself, or from the mythical constraints of that hideous Bell Jar. (Hence my worry about her influence on adolescent women poets.)

And yet you've also said 'being a writer proscribes role-playing'.
Which sounds rather more 'confessional' than I'd have expected. Even
your elegy 'Arioso Dolente' (Granny Scarecrow) seems unsentimen-
tal...

As Marianne Moore wrote (even Marianne Moore!) 'Poetry is
after all personal.' Even dramatic poetry carries the self-print of
the poet. Yes, my strongest impulse to write poems is personal
feeling and memory, which shouldn't really counteract impersonal perceptions or ideas. Here, again, form is the key. To write
in a form is to distance personal experience by making an art of
it. It's not that 'confession' cannot be informed by art; Seamus
Heaney's poems are full of his family life and memories, but they
are not self-indulgent because their startling language 'digs' them
into poems. 'Arioso Dolente' – a poem that means a lot to me –
is written in a form I worked out for it in the first stanza. Not
until I had that stanza down on paper did I know how to go on.
Other poets, mostly male (Yeats, W.H. Auden, Frost) showed me
the way.

For me your use of form – especially your range – marks you out.
I rarely write strictly according to 'rules', though when I do, I
keep them. But I enjoy playing with form; breaking the rules in
an original way to suit the poem in hand. A poem's theme or
subject usually determines its form. In this I believe poetry
requires of the poet as much mental discipline as mathematics
requires of the mathematician. The joy of making it is propor-
tional to the hard work put into it. Banality and sentimentality are
easy; they never question their own hackneyed ways.

So form acts as a kind of guarantor? Helps sift the 'real' from the
inauthentic, if you like?
Yes, I think so. Perhaps we should look at what Eliot meant by
'reality'. The question has always puzzled me. It's often used as if
it commanded general understanding, but it's actually an individual term. Every man's 'reality' is his own. For me, it has always
been the 'truth' about, as opposed to the appearance of, things,
beliefs, behaviours, events. Words have a way of inventing 'reali-

ties' instead of adhering to as much as we know of what happens. For me the question of what is 'real' and what is 'fiction' is at the heart of my poems, both impersonal and personal, whatever the form or style.

I'm not sure how confidently I could distinguish real from fiction, to be honest. But, yes, I accept that we carry our realities about with us; would Eliot agree? He's been important to you, hasn't he? I've tended to side with William Carlos Williams, down the years. But you have quite a bit in common with Eliot, really...

I'm not as devoted to Eliot as I once was. In an Eliot phase in my last years at University, I packed my memory with many of his lines, which resonate there better, I think than Williams'. But Eliot's Christian conclusions have never been mine, and I've felt companionable with Williams ever since I began discussing poetry with Lee Harwood and Ric Caddel in the 1980s.

I sense another kind of tension in your poetry, not unrelated to the reality/fiction thing, between thinking and feeling.

You mean the difference between poetry and logical analysis? Of course, it's been a factor in my relationship with my father, though I don't see why poetry shouldn't 'think'. All the finest English poets, Shakespeare through to Yeats, Stevens, Frost, found memorable language for thinking feelings. I can't believe thinking is not as emotional for a working scientist as for an imaginative writer. Imagination is a gift of the brain, after all; it has many mansions. There is no opposition between finding words for something actually observed and finding parallel images in metaphors, or even in fantasy.

No – but doesn't your poetry repeatedly discover how oppositions – real/fictional, then/now, human/environment – dissolve under the pressure of thoughtful attention? I'm thinking about those poems which watch people from a distance – like 'Binoculars in Ardudwy', or the holiday-makers on Harlech beach – which turn figures into shapes and patterns, like a kaleidoscope. But you can't take the interpreting eye out of the patterns it's imposed on contingency...

Yes, I agree with you entirely. The interpreting eye can never be left out of the equation. And, in a way, everything a person is, in his/her self, is a contingency. There never was a plan of life or of history or of nature kept rolled up in the sky, like a school map ready to be pulled down at a given time. And yet that contingency is, in fact, controlled at the roots by genetic selection and evolution. That's the paradox I find so interesting, living with my eyes open, waiting, without any pre-set theory of why or how, for what happens next.

Going back to reality then, would it be true to say that your Wales is your Wales, for example, and hang the stereotypes?
Well 'my Wales' isn't really my starting point, having in my various lives lived in so many places, in Britain and America. I'd say my Ardudwy is my Ardudwy because for twenty-eight years my English husband and I have been caretakers of the family's house in Cwm Nantcol. You can see it on the cover of my *Poems 1955–2005*. So I think Wales means, to me, the geological presence of the prehistoric landscape discovered and defined by Adam Sedgwick as Cambrian, and then (after quarrels with Roderick Impey Murchison) refined into Cambrian, Ordovician and Silurian. All these geological classifications happened in the 1830s, as described in my elegy, 'Cambrian'. It was the discovery, though my husband Peter, of geological Wales, that I'm sure has affected everything I have written since. Living in the Great Cwm (as Sedgwick named it in 1832) has completely changed the perspective and tenor of my poetry.

Your poem 'Stone Milk' talks about 'learning to find' a kind of consolation in landscape ('the milk of stones'); it seems – implicitly – more reassuring than human kindness. Yet the landscapes – the natural environments, mountains, weather, seasons – of your poems often seem like aggressors. So – an unsettling kind of solace?
I suppose so. 'Stone Milk', like many in that collection and my latest, *Astonishment,* is a response to getting older and feeling, with every year, less sensitive, less aware of loved places and people, less 'pushed' into poetry. But instead of resenting this

diminished sensibility, I feel from time to time, relieved, as if personal emotion were a burden too heavy for my ageing heart and mind. I've always derived a sense of liberation from knowing that insensible landscapes, geological formations, the tectonic flux of 'deep time' will survive, not only my own life and the present time, but the human species. And having no religious belief beyond awe that existence IS and can be amazingly felt and observed, I find comfort in a kind of withdrawal that enables me to comprehend more than my selfish troubles – such as they are. Uninhabited geology has become more important to me as I grow older, but the same attraction to self-absence (or self-effacement) can be found in one of my earliest poems, 'Sierra Nevada', which was written in the middle 1960s in California.

You don't care for critics, still less academics, as far as I can see. Why? You grew up in an academic household and you've worked in many universities over the years. What's wrong with academics, and/or (literary) criticism?

I've always had a love/hate affair with academia. When I was young, I needed to get away from it to appreciate its importance. I've since discovered that I can't live far from a university without missing university people as conversationalists. I have learned a lot, corresponding with academics; I think of friends like Philip Hobsbaum in Glasgow, Angela Leighton in Cambridge and Alasdair Fowler in Edinburgh; and many more over the years. In the Seventies, I was completely turned off by literary theory: Semiotics, Structuralism, Deconstruction; I feared that theory would eventually drive literature from the English curriculum. Now I worry that Creative Writing is taking over ground that would better be given to the study of language and other languages. I have long felt that English departments should be expanded into Departments of Comparative Literature, with an exhaustive programme of English poetry and fiction and a stiff requirement in at least two other languages. Mind you, I am preaching a doctrine of study that I avoided myself by being overly 'creative' during my four years at the University of Michigan. I suspect poets are good adjuncts to universities but they aren't often at home there. Randall Jarrell once wrote of a poet being like a pig wandering into a bacon factory: 'Go away, pig! What do you know about bacon?'

It's a great line. Thank you, Anne.

NERYS WILLIAMS

Nerys Williams grew up in Carmarthenshire. Her first full-length collection of poems, *Sound Archive*, was published to widespread acclaim by Seren in 2011. Williams is the author of *A Guide to Contemporary Poetry* (Edinburgh University Press, 2011) and *Reading Error: The Lyric and Contemporary Poetry* (Peter Lang, 2007) and numerous essays and articles in her specialist field of contemporary poetry. She has lived in the Republic of Ireland since 2002, where she holds a fulltime post lecturing in the School of English at University College Dublin.

Sound Archive *met with great enthusiasm when it appeared. Obviously you've been writing about contemporary poetry academically for years, but I hadn't realised just how much you wrote yourself. Was the collection long in the making?*
For a while academic writing took over a fair bit of what was visible of my writing in the public world. As a child I was always making phrases into these slightly-lopsided free verse spines down a page. Instinctively I gravitated towards free verse – although not completely unrhymed admittedly. My first 'real' poem (which I still have) was a response to Philippa Pearce's *Tom's Midnight Garden* when I was eleven. It was full of onyx, marble, grandfather clocks and taxidermy. Maybe not much has changed! After my teens I always kept a diary which I jotted things in, sporadically; I took the occasional creative writing class, but I was quite self-conscious when it came to reading my work out since it seemed very different, and I was dismayed at how little poetry was actually read by people taking poetry

classes. I defined myself as a reader first.

What kind of things were you reading? You're done with school, by now – how did you find your way towards the American avant-garde?
American Poetry hit me like a train when I was twenty. I'd always had an interest in modern poetry and I'd read all the obvious (Dylan Thomas, Eliot, Bishop, Plath and so on) and some perhaps not so obvious. Alun Lewis was a particular favourite. When I was twenty I entered an international programme at my home university of Stirling, and spent my third year in 1991 as an English Major at Berkeley. There I fortuitously stumbled into Robert Hass's lectures on contemporary poetry. Of course it being the Bay Area there were some remarkable poets still performing. I remember going to a reading in memory of Robert Duncan where Robin Blaser and Robert Creeley read. Thom Gunn's *The Man with Night Sweats* came out the same year. It led to a sustained interest in the poetry from the Bay Area and in contemporary poetry. I travelled across country with a copy of Donald Allen's *The New American Poetry* – it weighed a ton. It really was a remarkable year; the US felt very far from Carmarthenshire.

It sounds really generative. So those experiences helped propel you into academia, before you started writing yourself?
I followed my degree with an MA in Contemporary Poetry at Sheffield, then worked at BBC Wales for a while, before getting funding when Pete Nicholls, then at Sussex (now NYU) agreed to supervise my project on the lyric in late 20th Century American Poetry. When academic study took over, it seemed natural to use poetry to think through the dilemmas I was encountering in my research. I've always responded to poems I'm reading with a verse jotting in a diary, or a notebook entry. Many of the poets I was exploring, like Lyn Hejinian, Michael Palmer and Charles Bernstein, accompanied their poetry with essays which in themselves were forms of poetic writing. A Tŷ Newydd course in the late nineties run by Hilary Llewellyn-

Williams and Robert Minhinnick gave me some confidence; Robert generously took three poems for *Poetry Wales* that year. I 'returned' to poetry, consciously so to speak, when I started my first academic post in Ireland at TCD. I was having to perform far more to an Irish audience while lecturing and found I enjoyed reading out poems and introducing new poets to undergraduates. My next poems distilled some of my experiences working as an agency care assistant on psychiatric wards after completing my PhD (many eventually made their way into *Sound Archive*). I kept a notebook of jottings, and my partner Myles encouraged me to send work out. But looking back the breakthrough was winning the *Poetry Ireland* Ted McNulty Prize. It came out of the blue in an email; you can't apply – it's awarded to the best poem published by an Irish or Irish-resident poet in *Poetry Ireland Review* at the end of an editorship. The poem is called 'The Dead Zoo' and uses the National History Museum in Dublin as a space to perform an elegy for John Peel. And then there was a pause – I wanted to amass as much writing as possible before thinking of a volume. I also had quite an ambitious sense of how the architecture of a poetry volume should perform.

What do you mean?
I suppose I feel a collection should be quite an intricate thing – amassing a series of correspondences between poems, not only offering us reflections on established pre-existent spaces but also presenting us with imagined ones. Charles Bernstein's essay 'The Book as Architecture' describes the poetry volume as creating the blueprint for imagined spaces one has yet to encounter.[1] These spaces can of course be dreamscapes – I'm not suggesting I'm a civil planner! The performance is not only the speaking voice (or voices), but how the poems interact with one another. How a riff from one might be moved in a different direction in another.

And the ambition?
Well I was tired of reading first volumes where you could see the title poem approaching you with flashing lights. I tried to push form as far as I could in the space of a couple of pages.

Sometimes it works, sometimes maybe not, but I certainly didn't want a row of neat one-paged lyric poems. While an archive necessitates order, it also holds difference.

I can see what Sound Archive *does with that idea, and with dis/ordering all kinds of experiences and stories. But it also somehow turns sound itself – the sonic possibilities of text – into a kind of space ...*

I was thinking about the literal space of the BBC Sound Archive in Cardiff where I'd worked some years beforehand. The experience of cataloguing sound certainly was filtered through in the poetry. But the big shift was the move to Ireland in 2002. For a while I wrote sporadically, often revisiting spaces such as the six months at Berkeley on a Fulbright. These reflections all coalesced with a working-through of voices and losses, but when it came to putting the volume together in 2009-10 I edited quite fiercely. I wanted the book to sing in different voices and many textures. A period of great productivity the year before publication left me feeling quite stubbornly that I wanted the volume to reflect new work and new reading. So the whole process started some years before the collection appeared in 2011...

Are you conscious of handling recent poems in different ways? I'm wondering whether any new collection will get pared-back, or take you in an entirely fresh direction?

In musical terms that difficult second album? In the past couple of years I have been fascinated, if not obsessed with, a manmade island in San Francisco Bay called Treasure Island. It was originally conceived as a space in which to host the 1939-40 Golden Gate International Exhibition. Themes for the Fair were Pacific Unity, Peace and Innovation, and geographically the island is framed by the Golden Gate Bridge, the Bay Bridge and Alcatraz, so to some extent it is framed by reminders of Roosevelt's New Deal.

Treasure Island has catapulted my writing into a couple of different directions. I found masses of information and documentation while digging around in UC Berkeley's Bancroft

Library. The range of ephemera is fascinating – I've gravitated more and more to the oddities of the fair, for example the incubator babies on display as part of the science exhibition, the sponsored fruit and nut days, and the nude ranch in the more racy section of the island, which is incidentally named the Gayway. I've also been looking for a vocabulary to address what I've seen happen in Ireland during our recession, or what others would call depression. The locating of Ireland as Europe's once magic island of economic wizardry seems to marry well with the illusionary promises of a World's Fair in the 1930s. And strangely Treasure Island hosted its own Welsh Eisteddfod with a chairing ceremony and a druidic parade.

Crikey! So we're heading into time as well as place...
The key question has been how to assimilate these histories into poetry without killing it. I've found myself returning to how writers from the 30s used poetry to, as Muriel Rukeyser prophetically said, 'extend the document'; I'm thinking of how objectivist's like Louis Zukofsky, George Oppen and Carl Rakosi, and the wonderful Lorine Niedecker, responded to politics in their work. (Of course Oppen exchanged writing for political activism for a period). But balancing my gravitational pull towards lyricism in this mass of documentation has been a difficult balancing-act. I've found myself writing so-called found poems –they can seem gimmicky, but they're fun to perform! So my 'The Fiscal System and the Polluter Pays Principle' jostles with the titles of discarded books left outside economist Professor Colm McCarthy's office at UCD. I was interested in the books that he was happy to throw away.

But I've also been thinking about the recent debates concerning ideas of originality (Goldsmith, Perloff et al). I think poetry is asking some serious questions about its own form at the moment and perhaps more urgently about its role as credible commentator. Whether or not there's an audience for what I might call my 'collapsed lyric' is another matter. But I don't want new work to read as a testing-out, or a performing-of, rhetorical positions.

What do you mean by that phrase, 'collapsed lyric'?
It's a self-coinage (prompted by recent reflections) which I
suppose I'm using to describe a breaking-down of lyrical expec-
tations. Michael Palmer talks about an 'analytic' lyric which he
calls a reconstruction of human speech. In a post-second world
war poetic, the analytic lyric is not only highly self-reflexive but
attuned to the conditions of its own making – it doesn't take
human speech for granted but points us towards the mechanics
of language, towards how speech is in effect constructed. Often
poetry aims to show us the power relations that are performed in
speech. It could be thought of as the analysis of utterance. I'm
not claiming that for my own work – but let's take the premise of
a collapsed lung and a labouring for breath and articulation
(perhaps Juliana Spahr's *this connection of everyone with lungs* is
also at work here): I'm trying to evoke that pressure on the lyric
voice. You could think of it as the expanding and collapsing
bellows of an accordion, which sometimes produces a cacophony
of dissonance and competing notes, and often only the insistence
of one solitary tone. I guess I'm trying to find a term that moves
us away from Bakhtinian ideas of polyphony while avoiding
taking a single speaking voice for granted.

*So it's to do with how we make sounds, the layers of sound in
language, with our voices. You want the poem to escape any sort of
simplifying of the production of speech?*
Yes. I think that poetry is obviously terribly aware of the
processes of its making. But at its most basic there were a lot of
people that I lost during the time of writing the entire volume. I
wanted the book to offer not only a blueprint of imagined spaces
(if you think of the archive as architecture) but also all those lost
voices of family and friends. But I didn't want to collapse the
anecdotes and memories into singular self-reflection 'upon the
past' or offer voices in a clumsy way, like: *here comes the dialect,
folks...* Those voices needed to be activated and made synchro-
nous with the process of writing itself. So the closing lines from
the last poem of *Sound Archive*, 'Take me to the Columbarium',
came from a letter from one of my dearest friends, Cliff

Anderson, who was a jazz pianist. His words are put into an entirely different context (a San Francisco rococo mausoleum and reflections on war), but I hope made immediate, sagacious and mischievous at the same time.

You've talked a bit about performing. Do you find the space of the page restricting? A challenge?

In thinking about composition I'm always guided by the poems that I love, and return to – they're often longer poems or serial poems. I'm really captivated by the promise of unfolding in a long poem which isn't motivated by a more conventional sense of narrative, but is created through reiteration, rethinking, wandering and digression. A small lyric can also be a powerful thing, but some of the most powerful contemporary works have even the smallest lyrics reflecting back and forth upon one another within a volume. I know I keep coming back to the idea of the volume as an idealised book – which is perhaps something that is already anachronistic given the problems with publishing and the appetite for faster fixes in general. But let's take the LP and what's happened to the idea of the concept of an album. With downloads, as well as artwork we lose context and memory, in an odd way. I've grown up with that pleasurable anticipation of the next track on a familiar album: of knowing that the painful lyrical beauty of 'While my guitar gently weeps' is followed by the anarchy of 'Happiness is a Warm Gun', say, on *The White Album*. Of course that takes us onto the sticky ground of comparing music and poetry – I'm not a musician after all; I'm a poet! But one thing I've learnt through embracing editing is to trust my ear. The restriction of the page is a challenge but the distillation that can happen on that page (when it works) can make the hairs stand up on the back of your neck. As both practitioner and reader.

You say you're not a musician, but this conversation has been haunted by music in some ways. Like your poetry. I know how important music has always been to you – you've always been very involved in the contemporary music scene in Wales. So, do you play? Why didn't

you become a full-time musician?
I was in a concept band in my first year at Stirling: we never got beyond the concept, but the band members did write notes to one another about our ideas – which I've kept somewhere. It was a kind of anti-band in many ways. It would be quite difficult not to have had some appreciation of music from my traditional west Walian background, which was chapel-singing, school choirs and shows. I was even in a Welsh *cerdd dant* group that won at the National Eisteddfod! But I think the political charge happening with Welsh language music when I was a teenager was what made the difference. You had the distillation of punk through many bands – most explicitly Yr Anhrefn, then others like Traddodiad Ofnus, Y Cyrff, and Ffa Coffi Pawb – while Llwybr Llaethog were the first electronic dub reggae Welsh band ever. Of course a major influence would have been Datblygu. I remember seeing David R Edwards sampling a hair dryer on stage in Pontardawe (in 1988) and using that as part of the performance before playing a song called 'Cristion yn y Kibbutz', or 'Christian in the Kibbutz'. Crucially Cymdeithas yr Iaith (The Welsh Language Society) arranged gigs and often transport in rural areas to venues where you could hear live music. This really generated a sense of event – and fostered a DIY ethos. I loved scouting around charity shops and cutting out dresses from oversized 60s psychedelic clothes or old fashioned farmhouse aprons: there was this sense of making things to fit the event. What was specifically important about these bands was that they all wanted to problematise what it meant to be Welsh. But most of the bands I was interested in got their kudos from a less conservative music press and broadcasting opportunities in England. Like many teenagers in the 80s, I remember listening to John Peel in my bedroom and being so chuffed when he'd play a Welsh language band. That sense of being acknowledged elsewhere was really, really important. And it was reaffirmed when I went to Scotland when I was eighteen and found Welsh bands were known by non-Welsh speaking friends that I'd made. Those bands were trailblazers for a generation of musicians growing up in Wales. They promoted such a positive and open-ended sense of what

being Welsh was about – but tragically couldn't make a comfortable living from their music.

Music weaves itself in and through all the ideas you explore. As if, for you, the subject is constructed as much by music, or the sonic at least, as by language itself.

The ancient quarrel between conditions of music and poetry... Maybe music is the upper limit that every poet is striving towards. I think my interest in music has always informed my interest in lyricism, even the basic idea of the lyric poem as being traditionally accompanied by music. My range was extended by my friendship with Cliff, who taught me how to *listen*, to everything from Buddy Rich and Sarah Vaughan to Arvo Pärt and Beethoven's String Quartets. Of course my poetry doesn't just bear the intertextual resonances of music I listened to – although I'd love to recreate something similar to Steve Reich's 'Variations for Winds Strings and Keyboards' before I die! The poetry that I really love does use sound patterns, sonic accumulation and repetition to alert the reader to the strangeness of language or even the everyday. I often find that if I'm stuck, writing with music helps in abandoning self-reflection; it allows ideas to move. Sometimes I'm not even aware of the internal rhymes I'm creating; I just go by the momentum. I was very much taken with Caitlin Thomas' account of Dylan's working practices. Apparently she'd know if he was having a good day by his intoning in the shed, as she walked past on her way from The Boathouse to the main street. I think many critics have brushed over Dylan's musicality as pure glossolalia – which has often been a derogatory context. And growing up in St Clears, near Laugharne, Thomas' compound adjectives and absolute pleasure or *jouissance* with words is something that I was sympathetic to as a young reader.

Welsh was your first language. Do you think that ancient knotting of language and identity had anything to do with your shaping as a writer, perhaps not only as a poet?

I think that bilingualism informs the shaping of my work; I wrote a little bit about this a couple of years ago in *Poetry Wales*. Bilingualism offers a cultural awareness of linguistic perform-ance, which really helps or informs the writing of poetry. For example in rehearsing the performance of a poem, or the recital of a song, Welsh speakers occasionally gesture at a process of '*lliwio'r darn*', literally the 'colouring of the text'. But this expres-sion has little to do with 'filling in' a blank outline: it emphasises the tonal structure of the poem or lyric; how certain resonances can be accentuated through the modalities of voice. I think that's been a big influence. And some sense of 'outsider status' really helps with being confident enough to experiment and try differ-ent guises. I went to a Welsh language secondary school that was outside the catchment area when it really wasn't hip to do that. This was fifteen years or so before *Cŵl Cymru* and my affilia-tions to Welsh were tested by the more anglophile kids in my neighbourhood. It wasn't unusual to be shouted at as a 'Welsh Nash'. As a result I've always felt I have nothing to lose. I really do think that knowing more than one language teaches adaptabil-ity and gives you an openness to shifting gears from early on. I witness this every day with my two year old being raised as a Welsh speaker in Ireland. She already understands that she has to act as translator to some of the phrases we share – and this brings with it I think a sense of responsibility which is quite amazing to see in someone so young. Welsh is certainly the language of our skypeworld so, moving beyond the more obvious analogies of my being alert to Welsh poetic forms like *cywydd* and *englyn*, Welsh has become seriously linked in our house with twenty-first century communication. We even have *Cyw* beamed into our sitting room. Welsh is also now affiliated to a whole world of commercial enterprise from car number plates to bread bins!

Can you speak Gaelic?
No!

Has your Welshness made Ireland, with all its cultural complexities, feel more comfortable for you?
Certainly I have an affinity for the landscape which is very evoca-

tive of the West Wales I grew up in. The sense of humour resonates with me as does the idealism of community present in the county I've settled in – Co Meath. And in Ireland generally I've found books and readings particularly valorised and important to the cultural fabric of the country. However I think that there's an over-romanticisation of Irish radicalism in Wales. That was the biggest shock for me – how conservative a country it really is – and how dominated by parish pump politics. One key difference from Wales is obviously the relationship between state bodies or secular institutions and the influence of the church. Medical treatment, particularly female health, can be coded for the unwitting patient by the belief systems and doctrines of the church. You only have to think about the despicable treatment and death of Savita Halappanavar. It's no wonder that the early Irish feminist movements coined the slogan 'Keep your rosaries off our ovaries'. Successive Irish Governments have been generally reluctant to legislate for important issues such as fertility treatment, medical intervention during pregnancy and of course medical abortion. They know it raises the hackles of a very powerful pro-life lobbying group, but it also places doctors in an unenviable position. Of course the Church was also heavily involved in the provision of education, but this has changed and there is a very popular provision of school under the banner of 'educate together' promoting a secular approach which has spread well beyond Dublin.

On many levels Ireland has had to shift from nineteenth century values to a postmodern culture without the modern legislative markers that happened in other countries. Look how excavating the past has unearthed such traumatic histories of child abuse. But the Irish also have a remarkable resilience which I admire. We're trying to fix and acknowledge so many important things: psychic hurt and abuse, enabling immigrants as citizens, gay rights not to mention addressing the impacts of our financial collapse.

You're interested in politics, as this interview has underlined; I'm assuming that you'd be quite comfortable describing yourself as a feminist?

Yes. Some days I think working in academia that much has been achieved – and then other days I shudder how little has. Particularly to do with parenting and child-rearing. For example my maternity leave although covered by the state wasn't covered by a full time replacement, only by hourly paid teaching. This really is an erosion of how women are perceived in the workplace. And then we have courses proudly entitled gendering the canon, gendering the modern etc.! It would be difficult to live in Ireland and not be aware of the inequalities that still exist. But I'd never see politics and gender issues as distinct. I've always been political from an early age, having an interest in Cymdeithas yr Iaith and animal rights campaigns as well as taking part as a hunt saboteur in Scotland. But pregnancy really woke me up. I found myself quite proud to be strutting around the lecture theatre with a bump; showing it can be done. Or even increasing the visibility of the 'confinement' period in a public way.

How far did your mother help influence any of this? Did she work?
My mother and grandmother instilled in me the belief that education was a way into a career and independence. I was the first to go to University from both sides of the family. And this was due to their encouragement, I have no doubt. My grandmother was a diplomatic shopkeeper who was more or less a lone parent since she was widowed young. My mother is a fiercely independent thinker, as stubborn as a donkey over her beliefs. I hope I've inherited some of her tenacity and my Grandmother's diplomacy. She worked as a nurse when I was growing up and specialised as a community midwife, taking her exams while I was five. The midwifery course was residential so my father took a burden of childcare that year – which wasn't easy in the 70s and when he was working shifts in a creamery. I also travelled around the district with my mum during summer holidays. Her car was fascinating for a 10 year old: vacuum sealed sterile bandage packs, IUD coils, gas and air… It would be a health and safety issue these days. My father however also offered an important role – since he taught me poetry recitation for competitions when I was very small. And I grew up with a cupboard full of silver

cups won by him at local eisteddfods for recitation. My father's help with the childcare was crucial, since my mother's post was very erratic – she did home deliveries as well as hospital births and was often out all night.

Some of this is in the poetry, nor is it buried in the critical prose, but it's never very overt. Are you conscious of skirting it, or is it less deliberate?
I think there is a volume in there somewhere – but I'm always a bit superstitious about projecting about works which may never arrive. However I've stopped my mother from throwing out all her midwifery manuals. I want to try and combine some of the text with anecdotes (could be poetic prose) of her stories. Some are amazing – such as the baby that was born on the toilet and named Pan, or the father who cut the umbilical cord with his teeth while the dog ate the placenta. There seems to be such a lack of sharp, reflective writing about birth with a critical eye towards the pedagogy of childbirth and childrearing. In Ireland they're now paranoid about the small percentage of mothers that are breastfeeding – there's a lot of talk but very few facilities for the breastfeeding mum once she enters public space. I grew up with 'Breast is Best', but so little practical support exists. Much of the work I've encountered dealing with the realities of childrearing can seem saccharine or at worst quite narcissistic. There's this deficit in the market, so to speak; I think it's what compelled poet Andrea Brady to write *Mutability* (2012), which deconstructs childbirth and infancy. I'm also a fan of Laynie Browne's *Daily Sonnets* (2007), which were written during moments snatched while nursing and caring for a small child.

You've mentioned a few (wonderful) women writers; apart from Niedecker could you identify any particular significant influences?
Increasingly when I am stuck or thinking through ideas I find myself turning to contemporary American women poets – two key influences would be Jennifer Moxley and Juliana Spahr. They're very different writers. Moxley fashions her work from a tradition of European lyricism and I adore the sound of her work

– the sensation is of measuring, reflecting and discussing ideas without clumsiness. She shows us that sound is important. Her *Imagination Verses* and *The Sense Record* are pivotal to my library. Spahr offers a particular leisure and accretion that I find much sustenance in – creatively and politically. Her work struggles to address politics without reducing politics to something divorced from everyday life. In Wales Gwyneth Lewis has been a guide and her work an inspiration as a writer of Welsh and English. It has on occasion felt a little lonely being a Welsh poet writing in English in Ireland but her work reminds me that there are all kinds of directions a Welsh woman poet can take.

What kind of part has Wales itself, its very rich poetic heritage, played in your writing? Those ancient forms you just touched on – cywydd and englynion – are you aware of turning to them, or is it easier to turn away?
I've never really embraced formal metrics but I think the awareness of rhyme must be deep in my chiming self-conscious. I grew up memorising Welsh poetry, some mesmerising psalms from the Welsh Bible, *englynion*, and of course learning how to parse lines and identify differences between *cynghanedd groe*s and *sain* for example. I certainly think Welsh culture at large has had a linguistic and idiomatic impact on my writing. I'm particularly drawn to the poetry of T.H. Parry Williams and his adaptation of modernist forms. His work's provided a cue for adaptations such as 'Jezebel' in *Sound Archive* and more recently a poem called 'Clearing Space' after his 'Ymwacâd' (which I've adapted in reference to Ireland's 'Ghost Estates'). I'm very much drawn to the idea of adaptation and am keen to learn from the Welsh. But this direction is fairly recent.

Can you see yourself coming back to Wales, one day?
I'm raising a child in Welsh so we return to visit as often as we can. I think I might return but not for a considerable time. I'm fully aware that the West Wales I grew up in has changed significantly, and I am worried about the decline of Welsh in my native Carmarthenshire. There's no doubt that something in me is

attracted to a position of liminality. Being a Welsh writer in another country can mean one gets overlooked a little, because one isn't seen as a 'presence' – or as part of a network. However it also enables you to breathe a little and test out experiments. I think that it can protect against a certain laziness. Certitudes of place are more tempered. It's nice to flirt between two countries.

Many thanks, Nerys.

1. Charles Bernstein, 'The Book as Architecture: An Afterword', Michael Hinds and Stephen Matterson eds. *Rebound: The American Poetry Book*, Amsterdam: Rodopi, 2004. pp197-98.

SAMANTHA WYNNE-RHYDDERCH

Samantha Wynne-Rhydderch has produced three full-length collections of poetry: *Rockclimbing in Silk* (Seren, 2001); *Not In These Shoes* (Picador, 2008); and *Banjo* (Picador, 2012); she has also authored the pamphlet *Lime and Winter*[1] (Rack Press, 2014). She lives in New Quay, West Wales where she runs a writers' retreat, www.writebythecoast.co.uk.[2]

Can we start with your latest collection, Banjo, *and specifically 'Erratics', about life on the pioneering expeditions to Antarctica led by Ernest Shackleton and Robert Falcon Scott (Discovery 1901-1904, Terra Nova 1910-1913 and Endurance 1914-1916)*
Well the collection falls into two quite neatly balanced halves; the first half is a pathway to 'Erratics' in that all the speakers in those poems are on journeys. They wander from France to Hong Kong to Holland to North America to Dorset. The opening poem in the second half is titled 'The Piano', which prefigures the musical theme of the Antarctic sequence.

How did 'Erratics' come about?
The Discovery museum in Dundee has a photograph of some of the crew on the 'Discovery', dressed up as black and white minstrels. I started thinking about what all these middle class white men were doing in the coldest place on earth dressed as minstrels. I discovered that Leonard Hussey (the meteorologist and banjo player on 'Endurance') had just returned from a stint in the Sudan before going straight out the Antarctic; and I realised that part of what kept these men going in a difficult

environment was pretending to be somebody else. I immediately empathised because that's what I'm like. Part of what keeps me going is pretending to be somebody else through my poems.

Banjo *seems very much about method and process. It feels quite different from* Not In These Shoes. *Was that always your intention? I'm just thinking that there's a poem about Scott in* Not In These Shoes...

I always try to have a poem which points to the next collection, so yes, 'Abandonata' signposts this new collection. But I actually started writing *Banjo* in 1999, a long time ago now. It's a story I always wanted to explore, to find the right words for. But after I started I wasn't sure I could really put myself into the shoes of the characters, so I put it down and began on what became *Not in These Shoes* instead. I tried, unsuccessfully, to find funding to go to Antarctica. It was only when I heard Stef Penney talk about how she had written *The Tenderness of Wolves* without going to Canada that I decided I could continue.

Scott himself hardly features at all in your poems; you seem more drawn to the people around him.

I'm very interested in community and in teams and how people work together or not; what supports them, what destroys them and how they uphold each other in challenging environments. And with my own seafaring background I've always thought of a ship as being its own little community, each member dependent upon the others. I wanted to explore the generosity of spirit which keeps the community running smoothly. I deliberately didn't want to speak in the voice of Scott or Shackleton. There were certain voices I did want to adopt: Clissold, the cook on Scott's Terra Nova expedition; George Marston, the artist on Shackleton's Endurance expedition, and Hussey himself.

Why those voices?

Because they're not heard. They're crucial to the story yet you hardly ever hear them mentioned. I found them through reading, really. I started off with Alfred Lansing's book *Endurance*, and then I started to see beyond the expedition and went on forays to the Scott Polar Institute in Cambridge to read unpublished diaries and letters and listen to audio interviews. Then it was as if I became part of the team and I found it very hard to let go.

It feels like a book that's taken a lot of detailed work...
It was very hard work. Reams of notes and cross-checking details but I always knew what I was looking for so it was panning for gold, really. I knew when I came across the little sparkly bits I could do something with them. There was no doubt in my mind.

To me, those kinds of 'little sparkly bits' help to underpin the whole collection: the creativity behind the mechanical problem-solving, mending, making-do...
I'm fascinated by mechanism. I'm always intrigued by how one gets from A to B, by process and by the different jobs and roles that people have. I like to explore that through words. But I had to find a balance. I wouldn't want the poem to be top-heavy with lists of stores on deck, or dates, or too much historical background. If a poem becomes too heavy historically, it isn't then about the language. I was walking a tightrope between how much you let on and how much you leave out or try to show in a different way. 'Ponting' (awarded second prize in the 2011 National Poetry Competition) isn't – as one journalist said – 'about Captain Scott at the Antarctic' at all! It's about 'Ponting': the person *and* the verb. It's about living in a community; about being a photographer used to working on land who finds himself up the rigging in the crow's nest, who set up three planks leaning over the side so he could photograph the ship from a particular angle; about throwing up and trying to develop photographs at the same time. It also explores his time on the ice, teaching members of the Pole party how to take photographs without him, on the final leg of the journey to the Pole.

Isn't there a risk that however rigorous or powerful your poem, you'll never compete with the sensationalism of their story?
Well I thought it was a risk worth taking, rightly or wrongly. I

think the poems are more about language than story; that the narrative is at the service of the language. In spite of all the work and the learning behind it I tried to preserve a lightness of touch.

Many of the poems are wonderfully droll. But you don't go easy on yourself. You've talked about how you prepare the ground ahead of beginning a new poem. It's methodical, meticulous grafting. It's not as if you sit beside a blank page waiting for inspiration...
No. I have various mechanisms for making sure that the page isn't blank by the time I start the poem. I divide the page into three. I start with two columns at the top, which are half a page long which leaves just half a sheet of A4. In the top left column I write out the 'story' of the poem, in words or stick figures or arrows or a kind of code i.e. a + b = c. I need to know who's there, and who's talking, and how they're going to change during the course of the story. That's sorted by the time I start writing. In the other column I lay out all the images, any terminology or vocabulary that I might associate with the subject, any lines that have come to mind, and any research that I might have done. By then I've filled half the page and the poem's much less scary.

How long does this take?
I normally do that in a morning. Once I've started, there's no way back. If I've got to the stage where I've drawn those lines on the page I can't leave my writing shed until I've written the poem and I wouldn't want to either.

How did you end up developing your poems in that way?
I'm always quite forensic in the way I go about things normally. I enjoy chewing over a subject, thinking of it from all angles and voices and researching different elements before I decide where to plunge in. I try not to leave any stone unturned in this. I don't use all the information that I will have amassed. That's the hard part: deciding what to include. When I write, I examine an object or a place just as I might sail round an island. From the sea you'll get a much better perspective of the island than you will from simply walking across it. You'll see that one part of the coast is

rugged so you can't land there, but a little further along you might find a sheltered cove where you can get ashore very easily. In a similar way, a person or a place can have two or three completely different sides to them, but they are all constituent parts of that person or place. This is what makes them exciting to write about, because there is always a surprise in store for both the writer and the reader. I want to sail round that metaphorical island before I start writing so that I'll sound as convincing as possible to my reader.

Is it exciting? It can't all be hard work?
No, of course – it's great fun! The sense of excitement is greater than the fear of risk. I am a linguistic risk-taker. It's built into my psyche. The challenge embedded in the poem is more important to me than a fear of writing on a particular subject. So in the final instance, I'm absolutely convinced that I should be writing these things and in this way and that it's worth it. Otherwise I wouldn't do it.

When you revisit your published work, do you ever want to change things?
No. The poems are from a time and a place. It would be odd if my poems didn't in some way represent my own journey as a writer. You can only write from where you are and with the life experience and skills at your disposal.

You went to Cambridge. What did you study?
Classics: Greek and Latin. When you spend three years looking at cultures from over two thousand years ago, through their own languages, you develop a fascination with examining subjects from the inside, I think. And because these languages are not your mother tongue you're always experimenting with saying this or that in a different way. Once you take on the mantle of the translator you can never return to your mother tongue with the same eyes. The whole experience gave me a broader view of my own culture and a desire to master more languages. So I think being a Classicist was a little step in the process of becoming a

poet. Another was living in France for three years. I set myself the goal of disappearing into the culture linguistically, partly because I'm quite shy but partly because I get a kick out of hiding behind a role or a character or a language.

You've used tango to talk about writing poetry – as if it's a physical process. Can you say more about the relationship between the poem and the body?
I love bodies. They are the primary way that we connect to the world we live in; all the joy and pain that comes with being human, living in a community or family or relationship. In some ways I think the different parts of the body mirror the different parts of the poem. Each section or detail of the text interrelates, like all the different muscles and bones inside us. So it matters how we represent that as writers, through our narrative.

Why?
Because it's the only thing we've got to go on, the only evidence of our presence in the world (until we leave it). Who we are is very deeply connected to the way we treat our bodies. Until I learned Alexander Technique I had no idea how intertwined our minds and bodies are. Now I can think myself into particular muscles or bones which I didn't even know I had!

This makes me think of the slippages I find everywhere in your poetry, and not just between the different kinds of 'meaning' of a single word. You seem to slip between dimensions, even between planes of experience, so a sight might turn into a taste or a physical sensation or sound.
Well, to me it's as if it's all happening at the same time: I hear and see experiences all at the same time, like a kind of whirlwind. I see them as patterns, not as words and I then have to go back onto a 'normal' plane and translate the patterns, the music into words. By experiences I mean both everyday conversations, incidents in history, lines and stories that I've read, maps I've pored over, flowers that I have admired. To me it's all one long drama and it's happening now. All in one line. And then I have the challenge of making the poem.

Your work does reveal your striving to get that complex – the whirl-wind – said. But I rarely hear an 'I' that I can easily construct as 'Samantha Wynne-Rhydderch'...

Part of me is in every poem. If I weren't wedded to each poem as I was writing it, then my reader would see each speaker as a fake. I want them to sound authentic, so I put myself into each one. For that moment when the poem passes through me I am completely one with it and then it's gone from me, yet a part of me remains there in those lines. I think that's true of dancing partners too.

'Writing becomes a requirement / a dial on the gauge of inevitability / each morning the ache unfurls' (that's from 'Report' in Rockclimbing in Silk*). I don't necessarily want to ascribe those words to the you sitting here with me, but the commitment to language (the 'ache') sounds very like you.*

I think that's right. I'm never not trying to write, even when I'm not writing. Every hour of every day I know there are these particular poems that I am going to write regardless of the challenges.

Being in the National Wool Museum has made me think about how often you've turned to fabric as subject and image. It seems to make sense to find you here, among the looms...

Well I grew up partly in Lancashire against the backdrop of the mills. I didn't know I would one day explore textiles in my writing but it's felt more inevitable as time goes by. My mother was an artist, both a painter and a collage artist. She taught art mainly, but she did paint in her spare time – not that she had very much with four children. But we had lots of textiles around the house when I was growing up and I've no doubt that part of my inter-est stems from a familiarity with sewing machines and fabric. Coming to the museum felt like coming home!

What interests you about textiles? The way a fabric feels or appears? Or what can be made out of it?

Both, I think. This museum is a little heaven to me: a whirlwind of colours and textures and machines in the same place. I've no idea how I am going to distil it all.

How much of a part do voices play in the whirlwind? So many of the poems in Banjo *are fabricated out of the spoken; some seem to come quite close to 'found' texts. So the poem itself turns into a kind of fabric, woven out of a pattern of voice(s)...*
Yes. When I hear a voice there is no doubt in my mind what the voice is and what it's saying and how I need to continue with it. I hear it in a key. I hear a musical line first of all. I can't always decipher the words, but that doesn't bother me, because I can always decipher the tenor of the musical line. As long as I've got that in the voice, I know I'll be okay. If I couldn't hear that line I wouldn't even start to write the poem.

And there can be more than a single voice in a poem; so you'd be listening for their different lines? And then weaving those into a single or perhaps collective pattern, a story or history, colloquial, unwritten or possibly even made up?
That's it. For me a poem is like making vinaigrette, with varying quantities of voices, given lines, history, one's own experience and imagined experience mixed together to create a new taste for the reader.

But you often seem as interested in disorder as pattern. I'm thinking of 'Ladies with Hammers' (Banjo) *here –*
My husband lived on the south coast of England for years – and he took me to Chesil Beach and to look at the fossils on Bridport beach. I'd heard of Mary Anning, of course, but it was only when I went to Bridport that she came alive for me. I was intrigued by her fascination with the strata of her landscape.

I was also intrigued by 'Hong Kong Mah Jong' (Banjo).
I wrote that poem after visiting Hong Kong with my sister Fran. We went out to see the place where my great-aunt had been interned by the Japanese as prisoner of war, and I felt drawn to explore our visit through Mah Jong. We had the game at home

but I only know the very basics; I was always intrigued by the engraved little tiles. Hong Kong felt unexpectedly familiar to me because so many of the souvenirs and little objects I saw there were ones that I have around the house, things which I've inherited. They were once at strange and familiar, which was quite unnerving. That was what I wanted to explore in the poem. I wove my great-aunt's experience into the final lines of the poem: before you start playing Mah Jong you have to build a four-sided city wall out of the tiles and then deal out a portion of the tiles to each player. This made me think of the prisoner of war camp where my great aunt had been and how weird it must have been, aged just twenty three, to have found yourself there faced by complex things you could do nothing about. She spent half her twenties incarcerated on the other side of the world.

Can we talk about the sea-faring family from New Quay. It sounds very romantic...
It wasn't; my father was in the Merchant Navy for years before he became Chief Fishery Officer at the South Wales Sea Fisheries Committee in Swansea. I think we moved eleven times by the time I was eighteen and I went to four different primary schools (although I was at the same secondary school). I'm not sure why we moved so much. I think my parents just liked houses! It's a love I have inherited. I'm fascinated by architecture and design. And it's given me a spirit of 'get up and go'. I could live anywhere and be happy in my little space.

When did you start thinking of writing as being important?
When I was about seven. It was just something I always did. There wasn't a moment when I suddenly thought, now I'm a writer. I think probably as a teenager I started to identify more with poetry than prose. I just assumed that all this writing was a teenage phase and that it would pass, but it didn't.

Did you all write?
If we went out for the day somewhere we'd write it up afterwards in our journals sitting round the table. So yes, it started as quite

a communitarian activity and then became a habit. A good habit.

And it was a big family, too. I'm wondering about that interest in community.
I suppose my role model for community was my parents' relationship: much of the time they didn't see each other because of my father being away at sea for all my early childhood. If you start off with that as a norm, it's possible for you to have quite an intense relationship with people you don't see all the time. There's the immediate family community, and there's also the historical family: the absent, the missing in action, who become alive through the stories handed down to you.

And Welsh? You're a Welsh speaker...
I learnt some Welsh at school but I only started learning it properly when I married my husband, Geraint, who is a mother-tongue Welsh speaker. My mother was a Welsh speaker but she didn't speak to me in Welsh, probably because I grew up partly in England.

Do you think of yourself as Welsh? Are you political?
I take it as part of the fabric of being me. I'm quite happy to be identified as a Welsh writer. I don't think of myself as particularly political but I am shocked if people tell me that they don't vote or have forgotten to vote. So I must care more than I realise. I can't imagine not voting, especially when women have had the vote for less than a hundred years. We owe it to those who fought so hard for our democratic freedom.

Can you say what you think of as being 'Wales'?
That's quite difficult to answer. Sometimes I've lived here, sometimes I haven't; I've always been inside and outside at the same time. As a teenager and in my twenties I was often told I didn't sound English or wasn't Welsh enough. Wherever I was I seemed to have the wrong kind of voice or accent. I think that helped me to develop voices: trying to fit in. You have to learn to adopt a particular way of speaking in order to survive

playground life, especially as a child. I'm sure that's been useful in helping me get into a voice or character.

Earlier you were talking about finding the 'story' of a poem. For me stories don't happen easily in the space of the poetic text except perhaps in longer, looser forms, like ballad.
I couldn't really entertain the idea of a poem that didn't somehow have a story to it. I'm fascinated by narrative. As a reader I want to know the story, to identify with the character and see whether they would react the way I would, given their circumstances. I think of it as the core of each poem really.

But stories are linear: you follow them along the line of continuous prose. Whereas poems set up different kinds of spatial relationships between words and lines, don't they? Poetry configures itself differently.
I find the fact that a poem is quite small and can only contain certain elements very exciting. I want to be able to tell the story within that; I find it really thrilling, having to choose the top three things out of all the stuff in my notes. It's so important not to feel compelled to use every idea you have.

And the form doesn't get in your way?
No, it encourages the narrative to go in unexpected directions; it requires me as a writer to 'up my game.' For example, a particular rhyme scheme in a poem can force the language to go down new syntactical avenues. I can't put into words what fun it is.

I think of you as an intensely formal writer.
I think I am. Once you start reading lots of sonnets, say, it gets into your bloodstream, and you start hearing those beats in the clickety-clack of your ordinary life. I tend to think in little blocks anyway, little blocks of colour. That's how I live my life, in tiny pages. What matters is what you can carry with you, in your head, what you can remember, what you have learned and reflected on. These are the things that make us what we are.

Is there a particular form that you especially enjoy?

I really do love the sonnet, but there are other forms which I wish I could inhabit in the same way but haven't yet mastered, for example the villanelle and the sestina and the ghazal.

You're good at couplets; does that have anything to do with your interest in alterity?
Yes. Getting into the different shoes. I feel constantly divided into two: there's the self I leave behind in the (writing) shed when the other self goes out to teach or give readings or hoover the house. The strange thing is that I know that the me that I leave in the shed is always writing, making notes, thinking about the next poem. There is no let-up, either for her or me. But at least she's getting on with the writing, even if I'm not there.

So each time you adopt a different voice, you need to find the best shape on the page for it. How do you do that?
Trial and error. I'll usually have an idea before I start. You can never be sure if it's going to work out, but it keeps my mind focussed on the form. I love patterns. There's something reassuring about knowing it's going to crop up again. I like everything to be completely ordered, on the table, the page, the wall.

Do you have an ideal reader in mind?
Oh yes I do. Me! And contemporary writers whose work I admire. That I'm a woman isn't the most important thing about me. It's like being born Welsh, or with pale skin. I don't give those things a second thought. But of course they impact on one's daily life. And as a reader I think you have to be attentive, to give yourself the chance to hear what the poem is doing and saying. You have to be prepared to let go as a reader, to give yourself up to the poem, to allow yourself to become the character in the poem, as you would in a novel.

Do you feel you've been misread?
I didn't realise how important gender was for some critics. I had no idea that some people would object to my writing about, well, apple pies! I've never made an apple pie but I didn't let that stop

me from imagining what it must be like to make one. For me, there can't be a topic which is off limits for writers, be it your own experience, or a made-up experience or that of an historical figure or a blend of all three. I still don't understand why it's problematic. Inescapably, we all write out of our gender, as man or as woman.

Some readings describe you as domestic, or domesticated; some call you a surrealist.
I wish I were more domesticated – I can hardly cook and barely sew! So if I give the impression of being good at either in my poems then the writing must be convincing. But I think I slip in and out of all those kinds of categories. I'm a bit Thetis-like: sometimes I'm surreal, sometimes very plain-speaking and sometimes I write through historical voices. The house of my head contains many rooms, and I love them all in different ways. I realise this makes it hard to pin my work down – its many selves – but I so enjoy moving in and out of different poetic spaces.

Are those selves always interested in some kind of process, or mechanism?
I do like to know the connections between things. How you get from here to there. I like to be in control of that. So I take lots of notes and spend ages working out narrative paths or how to repair a fridge. That aspect of my thinking is probably more developed in this collection, but I've been like that since I was very small.

Why the fascination with machines?
I'm completely useless with machines, and entranced by people who have an encyclopaedic knowledge of a subject and can delve into what they know to fix something. I've written off three cars. So, for the poem 'Dodge' I gave myself the task of getting into the head of this character who's repaired his Dodge truck. The only way was to know a lot about fixing 1940s and 1950s Dodge pickups. So I read quite a few manuals. My husband thought it was hilarious.

You're not techy then?
No [*laughing*]. I like to make out that I am, but I'm not. The trouble is that every time I read a manual I want to write a poem about it rather than fix whatever's broken.

The poem allows you to be things that you're not. Do you act?
No! I'm really shy; I just couldn't. It's more the voice I'm interested in. That's what I find exciting. That sort of Mr Benn-type situation where you can go in and put on the clothes and be that character for the poem. And, hopefully, the reader has that experience too, every time they read the poem.

Who do you read?
I love reading. I try to read a combination of books. I really love Wordsworth, Ted Hughes, Larkin, Elizabeth Jennings, Sinéad Morrissey, Matthew Hollis, and R.S. Thomas. Then there's a poet called Heather Phillipson, published by Faber... So, a combination of new and old.

People have heard Plath in your work.
I really love Plath. I'm sure she informs my writing, as she does all writers, but I wouldn't say that she has been a model for me. I'm more of an Elizabeth Bishop fan. Finding female models hasn't been important for me. I'm interested in good writing, regardless of the gender of the author.

Does any other art form come close to poetry for you?
In another life I would definitely have been a photographer. I love the camera – as long as I'm behind the lens, not in front of it. Also, interior design. Homes and gardens. Furniture and houses and rooms. My garden is, well, almost like a story in a poem, the story of the garden. My garden is very steep: it's split into four terraces, each with a different function, and each layer is to me a verse in a poem. There are elements in each terrace that point towards the next, each offers different ways of looking at the garden. The story of the garden isn't fully revealed until you reach the top terrace. I think of the poem like that. I like to keep

the reader blindfold as far into the poem as I can, and when the blindfold comes off it's quite exciting.

Thank you very much.

1. This pamphlet was the result of a residency at the National Wool Museum in Felindre Fach, Carmarthenshire, where this interview was held in 2012.
2. A shortened version of this interview appeared in *Poetry Wales* No. 48, issue 2 pp. 53-58.

ACKNOWLEDGEMENTS

Thanks are due first and foremost to the poets to whom this book owes its existence. It was never less than a delight and privilege to tour its different byways with interlocutors who made as grounded and interested witnesses of that process. I am indebted to them for the uncomplaining generosity with which each gave of her time, patience and intellectual energy. I hope the conversations as they appear here leave a palpable trace of the pleasure it has been for me to fall into step with so diverse and stimulating a company of creative artists.

I am likewise grateful to Mick Felton and the hardworking team at Seren for their good-humoured, imaginative and professional support of a project so long in the making. Finally, I want to thank my family and an assortment of long-suffering friends, for all kinds of specialist and often last minute assistance ranging from direction-giving to childcare. As ever Tom, on whose recording equipment the whole project depended in its early stages, has been a steady source of strength and technical know-how throughout.

WORKS CITED

Abse, Dannie. *Speak, Old Parrot*. London: Random House, 2013.

Allen, Donald. *The New American Poetry*. New York: Grove Press, 1960.

Atkinson, Tiffany. '99', *Catulla Et Al.* Tarset: Bloodaxe Books, 2011.
  Catulla Et Al. Tarset: Bloodaxe Books, 2011.
  'Hymen Hymenaeus', *Catulla Et Al*. Tarset: Bloodaxe Books, 2011.
  Kink and Particle. Bridgend, Seren, 2006.
  So Many Moving Parts. Tarset: Bloodaxe Books, 2014.
  (ed.) *The Body*. Basingstoke and New York: Palgrave Macmillan, 2005.

Balmer, Josephine. *Catullus: Poems of Love and Hate*. Tarset: Bloodaxe Books, 2004.

Barnes William. *Selected Poems*. Ed. Andrew Motion. London: Penguin Books, 1994.

Benjamin, Walter. *The Arcades Project*. Trans. Howard Eiland and Kevin McLaughlin. Cambridge, MA and London: Belknap Press of Harvard University Press, 1999.

Bernstein, Charles. 'The Architecture of the Book', *Rebound: The American Poetry Book*. Ed. Michael Hinds and Stephen Matterson New York and Amsterdam: Rodopi Books, 2004. pp. 195-198.

Bidgood, Ruth. 'All Souls', *The Print of Miracle*. Llandysul: Gomer, 1978.
  'At Strata Florida', *Not Without Homage*. Swansea: Christopher Davies, 1975.
  'Into the Dark', *The Fluent Moment*. Bridgend: Seren, 1996.
  'Llandewi Hall, Radnorshire', *The Given Time*. Swansea: Christopher Davies, 1972.
  'Not The Pathetic Fallacy', *The Fluent Moment*. Bridgend: Seren, 1996.
  'Omen', *New and Selected Poems*. Bridgend: Seren, 2004.
  'Shepherd's Cottage', *The Given Time*. Swansea: Christopher Davies,

1972.

'Singing to Wolves', *Singing to Wolves*. Bridgend: Seren, 2000.

'Strangeness', *The Fluent Moment*. Bridgend: Seren, 1996.

'The Green Man at Bwlch', *Selected Poems*. Bridgend: Seren, 1992.

'Valley-before-Night', *Selected Poems*. Bridgend: Seren, 1992.

Brady, Andrea. *Mutability: Scripts for Infancy*. Chicago: University of Chicago Press, 2013.

Bromwich, Rachel, ed. *Trioedd Ynys Prydein / The Welsh Triads*. Cardiff: University of Wales Press, 1961.

Browne, Laynie. *Daily Sonnets*. Denver, Colorado: Counterpath Press, 2007.

Burns Singer, James. *Selected Poems*. Ed. Anne Cluysenaar. Manchester: Carcanet Press, 1977.

Calvino, Italo. *Invisible Cities*. Trans. William Weaver. Italy: Giulio Einaudi, 1974

Carroll, Donald, ed. *New Poets of Ireland*. Denver: Alan Swallow, 1963.

Chamberlain, Brenda. *The Green Heart*. Oxford University Press, 1958

Chtcheglov, Ivain. 'Formulary for a New Urbanism'. *Leaving the 20th Century: The Incomplete Work of the Situationist International*. Trans and ed. Christopher Gray. London: Rebel Press, 1998.

Clarke, Gillian. 'The Sundial', *Collected Poems*. Manchester: Carcanet, 1997.

Cluysenaar, Anne. *Batu-Angas: Envisioning Nature with Alfred Russel Wallace*, Bridgend: Seren, 2008

'Clay', *Migrations*. Blaenau Ffestiniog: Cinnamon Press, 2011.

Migrations. Blaenau Ffestioniog: Cinnamon, 20011.

Timeslips: New and Selected Poems. Manchester: Carcanet, 1997.

Touching Distances. Blaenau Ffestiniog: Cinnamon Press, 2014

'Vaughan Variations', *Timeslips: New and Selected Poems*. Manchester: Carcanet, 1997.

Connor, Stephen. *Dumbstruck: A Cultural History of Ventriloquism*. Oxford: Oxford University Press, 2000.

Conran, Tony. *Penguin Book of Welsh Poetry*. Harmondsworth: Penguin, 1967.

Certeau, Michel de. 'Walking in the City'. *The Practice of Every Day Life*. Trans. S. Rendall. Berkeley: University of California Press, 1984.

Dowson, Jane and Alice Entwistle. *A History of Twentieth Century British Women's Poetry*. Cambridge: Cambridge University Press, 2005.

Elfyn, Menna. *Cusan Dyn Dall / Blind Man's Kiss*. Tarset: Bloodaxe *Cell Angel*. Newcastle Upon Tyne: Bloodaxe Books, 1996.

'A Door in Epynt', *Murmur*. Tarset: Bloodaxe Books, 2012.

Merch Perygl: Cerddi 1976-2011. Llandysul: Gomer, 2011.

'Neges' / 'Message', *Eucalyptus Detholiad o Gerddi 1978-1994 /
Eucalyptus: Selected Poems 1978-1994*. Llandysul: Gomer, 1995.
Murmur. Tarset: Bloodaxe Books, 2012.
*Perffaith Nam: Dau Ddetholiad & Cherddi Newydd 1995-2007 /
Perfect Blemish: New and Selected Poems 1995-2007*. Tarset,
Bloodaxe, 2007.
'Cân y di-lais i British Telecom' / 'Song of a Voiceless Person to
British Telecom', *Eucalyptus Detholiad o Gerddi 1978-1994 /
Eucalyptus: Selected Poems 1978-1994*. Llandysul: Gomer, 1995.
Entwistle, Alice. *Poetry, Geography, Gender: Women rewriting contempo-
rary Wales*. Cardiff: University of Wales Press, 2013.
Evans, Christine. 'Adjusting the Focus', *Growth Rings*. Bridgend: Seren,
2006.
'Bonanza', *Looking Inland*. Bridgend: Poetry Wales Press, 1983.
Burning The Candle. Llandysul: Gomer, 2006.
'Cometary Phases', *Cometary Phases*. Bridgend: Seren, 1989.
Cometary Phases. Bridgend, Seren: 1989.
'In Women's Thanatological', *Cometary Phases*. Bridgend: Seren,
1989.
'Latency', *Cometary Phases*. Bridgend: Seren, 1989.
Looking Inland. Bridgend: Poetry Wales Press, 1983.
'Unseen Island', *Looking Inland*. Bridgend: Poetry Wales Press, 1983.
'Weaning', *Looking Inland*. Bridgend: Poetry Wales Press, 1983.
Fisher, Catherine. *Immrama*. Bridgend: Seren Books, 1988.
The Box of Red Brocade. London: Hodder Children's Books, 2013
The Candleman. London: Red Fox, 2011.
The Obsidian Mirror. London: Hodder Children's, 2012.
Friedan, Betty. *The Feminine Mystique*. Harmondsworth: Penguin, 1965.
Gramich, Katie and Catherine Brennan, eds. *Welsh Women's Poetry
1460-2001*. Dinas Powys: Honno Classics, 2003.
Gramsci, Antonio. *Selections from the Prison Notebooks* ed. Quintin
Hoare. London: Lawrence and Wishart, 1998.
Green, Melissa. *The Squanicook Eclogues*. Boston, MA: Pen and Anvil
Press, 2010.
Grosz, Elizabeth. *Architecture from the Outside: Essays on Virtual and Real
Space*. Cambridge, MA: MIT Press, 2001.
Gunn, Thom. *The Man with Night Sweats*. London: Faber & Faber,
1992.
Heaney, Seamus. 'Act of Union', *North*. London: Faber & Faber, 1975
Field Work. London: Faber & Faber, 1979.
Henry, Paul. *The Brittle Sea*. Bridgend: Seren Books, 2010.
Hoffman, Eva. *Lost in Translation: A Life in a New Language*. London:

Penguin, 1990.

Johnston, Dafydd, Huw Meirion Edwards, Dylan Foster Evans, A. Cynfael Lake, Elisa Moras and Sara Elin Roberts, eds. *Cerddi Dafydd ap Gwilym* [*The Complete Poems of Dafydd ap Gwilym*]. Cardiff: University of Wales Press, 2010.

Jones, David. *Anathemata*. London: Faber & Faber, 2010.
    In Parenthesis. Introd. T S Eliot. London: Faber & Faber, 2010
    The Sleeping Lord and Other Fragments. London: Faber & Faber, 1995.

Koolhaas, Rem. *Delirious New York: A Retroactive Manifesto for Manhattan*. 1978. New York: Monacelli Press, 1994.

Krog, Antjie. *A Change of Tongue*. Cape Town, SA: Struik Publishers, 2009.
    Country Of My Skull: Guilt, Sorrow, and the Limits of Forgiveness in the New South Africa. Cape Town/London: Random House/Vintage, 1999.
    'Self-translation', *The Poetry Paper* 5 (2008/9) 21-22.
    'In The Name Of The Other: Poetry in self-translation' [www.litnet.co.za/Article/in-the-name-of-the-other-poetry-in-self-translation]

Lansing, Alfred. *Endurance: Shackleton's Incredible Voyage to the Antartic*. 1959. London and New York: Phoenix (Orion) 2000.

Lawrence, D.H. *Sons and Lovers*. 1913. Cambridge: Cambridge Univesrity Press, 1992.

Lewis, Gwyneth. *Keeping Mum*. Tarset: Bloodaxe Books, 2003.
    Sunbathing in the Rain. A Cheerful Book on Depression. London and Philadelphia: Jessica Kingsley Publishers, 2007.
    'Ynys', *Cyfansoddiadau a Beirniadaethau Eisteddfod Genedlaethol Bro Morgannwg 2012 / The Compositions and Adjudications of the National Eisteddfod Vale of Glamorgan 2012*.

Mandelstam, Nadezhda. *Hope Against Hope*. London: Atheneum Publishers, 1970.

McBreen, Joan ed. *An Phileog Bhan/The White Page: Twentieth-Century Irish Women Poets*. Cliffs of Moher, County Clare: Salmon, 1999.

Merrill, James. *The Changing Light at Sandover* [1980-82]. Ed. J D McClatchy and Stephen Yenser. New York: Alfred A. Knopf, 2011.

Meyrick, Ceri, ed. *The Bloodstream*. Bridgend: Seren Books, 1989.

Millett, Kate. *Sexual/Textual Politics*. London: Virago, 1977.

Monk, Geraldine. *Escafeld Hangings*. Sheffield: West House Books, 2005.

Mouré, Erin. *O Cidadán*. Toronto: Anansi, 2002.

Moxley, Jennifer. *Imagination Verses. 1996*. Cambridge: Salt, 2003.
    The Sense Record and other poems. 2002. Cambridge: Salt, 2003.

Mulford, Wendy. 'Alltud', *Scintilla*, 11 (2007): 153-61.

'I CHINA AM', *The Land Between*. Hastings: Reality Street, 2009.

'Notes on Writing: A Marxist/Feminist Viewpoint'. *On Gender and Writing*. Ed. Michelene Wandor. London: Pandora Press, 1983. pp. 31-41.

The East Anglia Sequence. Peterborough: Spectacular Diseases, 1998.

and Sara Maitland. *Virtuous Magic: Women Saints and their Meanings*. London: Mowbray, 1998.

Helen Kidd, Julia Mishkin and Sandi Russell, eds. *The Virago Book of Love Poetry*. London: Virago, 1990.

Olsen, Tillie. *Silences*. New York: Delacorte Press/Seymour Lawrence, 1978.

O'Sullivan, Maggie ed. *Out of Everywhere: linguistically innovative poetry by women in North America and the UK* London and Suffolk: Reality Street Editions, 1996.

Pearce, Philippa. *Tom's Midnight Garden*. Oxford: Oxford University Press, 1958.

Penney, Stef. *The Tenderness of Wolves*. London: Quercus, 2006.

Pugh, Sheenagh. *The Democratic Genre: fan fiction in a literary context*. Bridgend: Seren, 2005.

'Earth Studies', *Earth Studies and Other Poems*. Bridgend: Poetry Wales Press, 1982.

'Fanfic', *The Beautiful Lie*. Bridgend: Seren, 2002.

Folk Music. Bridgend: Seren 1999.

'Lady Franklin's Man', *The Beautiful Lie*. Bridgend: Seren, 2002.

'Regina', *Long Haul Travellers*. Bridgend: Seren 2008.

'The Arctic Chart'. *Stonelight*. Bridgend: Seren, 1999.

'The Big Sky', *Short Days Long Shadows*. Bridgend: Seren 2014.

'The Boyhood of Tristan Jones', *Long Haul Travellers*. Bridgend: Seren 2008.

Short Days Long Shadows. Bridgend: Seren 2014.

'Walsingham's Men', *Short Days Long Shadows*. Bridgend: Seren 2014.

'Webcam Sonnets', *Long Haul Travellers*. Bridgend: Seren 2008.

Long Haul Travellers. Bridgend: Seren 2008.

Rees-Jones, Deryn. *Burying the Wren*. Bridgend: Seren, 2012.

Quiver. Bridgend: Seren, 2004.

Robertson, Lisa. *Occasional Work and Seven Walks from the Office of Soft Architecture*. Astoria, OR: Clear Cut Press, 2003.

Samuels, Lisa. *Gender City*. Exeter: Shearsman, 2011.

Sapir, Edward. *Language: An Introduction to the Study of Speech*. London:

Hart-Davis, 1963.

Sheppard, Robert. *Far Language: Poetics and Linguistically Innovative Poetry, 1978-97.* Exeter: Stride Publications, 2002.

Skoulding, Zoë. *Contemporary Woman's Poetry and Urban Space: Experimental Cities.* London: Palgrave Macmillan, 2013

'Forest with A to Z of Cardiff', *Remains of a Future City.* Bridgend: Seren, 2008.

Remains of a Future City. Bridgend: Seren, 2008.

'The house where it is impossible not to fall in love', *Remains of a Future City.* Bridgend: Seren, 2008.

The Mirror Trade. Bridgend: Seren, 2004.

The Museum of Disappearing Sounds. Bridgend: Seren, 2013.

'The noble and tragic quarter', *Remains of a Future City.* Bridgend: Seren, 2008.

Ingmara Balode, Julia Fiedorczuk, Sanna Karlström, Ana Pepelnik, Sigurbjörg Þrastardóttir, and Elzbieta Wójcik-Leese. *Metropoetica – Poetry and urban space:Women writing cities.* Bridgend: Seren, 2103.

Somerville-Arjat, Gilleán and Rebecca E. Wilson, eds. *Sleeping with Monsters: Conversations with Scottish and Irish Women poets.* Edinburgh: Polygon, 1991.

Spahr, Juliana. *this connection of everyone with lungs.* Berkeley: University of California Press, 2005.

Stephens, Meic ed., *Poetry 1900-2000.* Cardigan: Parthian / Library of Wales, 2007.

Stevenson, Anne. 'Arioso Dolente', *Granny Scarecrow.* Tarset: Bloodaxe, 2000.

Astonishment. Tarset: Bloodaxe Books, 2012.

Bitter Fame. London: Penguin, 1990.

'Cambrian', *Poems 1955-2005.* Tarset: Bloodaxe, 2000.

'New York', *Poems 1955-2005.* Tarset: Bloodaxe, 2000.

Poems 1955-2005. Tarset: Bloodaxe, 2006.

Selected Poems. New York: Library of America, 2008.

'Sierra Nevada', *Living in America.* 1965. *Poems 1955-2005.* Tarset: Bloodaxe, 2000.

'Stone Milk', *Stone Milk.* Tarset: Bloodaxe Books, 2007

Tarlo, Harriet, ed. *The Ground Aslant: An Anthology of Radical Landscape Poetry.* Exeter: Shearsman, 2011.

Thomas, R.S. 'The Island Boatman', *Uncollected Poems.* Ed. Tony Brown and Jason Walford-Davies. Northumberland: Bloodaxe Books, 2013.

Thompson Seton, Ernest. *Wild Animals I have Known.* New York: Scribners, 1912.

Williams, Gwyn. *The Burning Tree: Poems from a Thousand Years of Welsh*

Verse. London: Faber, 1956.

Williams, Nerys. 'Jezebel', *Sound Archive*. Bridgend: Seren, 2011.

 Sound Archive. Bridgend: Seren, 2011.

 'Take Me to the Columbarium', *Sound Archive*. Bridgend: Seren, 2011.

 'The Dead Zoo', *Sound Archive*. Bridgend: Seren, 2011.

Williams, William Carlos. *Paterson*. New York: New Directions, 1963.

Wynne-Rhydderch, Samantha. 'Abandonata', *Not In These Shoes*. London: Picador, 2006.

 Banjo. London: Picador, 2012.

 'Dodge', *Banjo*, London: Picador, 2012.

 'Erratics', *Banjo*, London: Picador, 2012.

 'Hong Kong Mah Jong', *Banjo*. London: Picador, 2012.

 'Ladies with Hammer', *Banjo*. London: Picador, 2012.

 Not In These Shoes. London: Picador, 2006.

 'Ponting', *Banjo*. London: Picador, 2012.

 'The Piano', *Banjo*. London: Picador, 2012.

INDEX

THE EDITOR

Alice Entwistle is Principal Lecturer in English at the University of South Wales. She has published widely on mid-century and contemporary Anglo-American poetics, latterly concentrating mainly on those working in or identifying with the devolved regions of the United Kingdom, and frequently on women. She co-authored *A History of Twentieth Century British Women's Poetry* (Cambridge, 2005) with Jane Dowson, and contributed essays to *A Cambridge Companion to British and Irish Women's Poetry* (ed. Dowson 2011), *A Cambridge History of English Poetry, The Edinburgh Companion to Scottish Literature* and *A Cambridge Companion to Sylvia Plath.* Her most recent publication is *Poetry, Geography, Gender: Women Rewriting Contemporary Wales* (University of Wales Press, 2013).